THE LEGACY
of the
TEK SING

的 惺

THE LEGACY
of the
TEK SING

*China's Titanic – its Tragedy
and its Treasure*

Nigel Pickford & Michael Hatcher

with a section on the porcelain by
David Freedman

GRANTA EDITIONS

Published by Granta Editions, 25–27 High Street,
Chesterton, Cambridge CB4 1ND, UK
Granta Editions is a wholly owned imprint of Book Production Consultants plc

First published in 2000

A CIP catalogue record for this book is available from the British Library.

ISBN 1 85757 069 3

Design by Tim McPhee
Design and production in association with
Book Production Consultants plc, 25–27 High Street,
Chesterton, Cambridge CB4 1ND, UK
http://www.bpccam.co.uk

Printed and bound by Clifford Press, Coventry, UK
Colour origination by Lithocraft, Coventry, UK

Frontispiece: Porcelain from the Tek Sing *with coral growth.*
(Nagel Auctions, Stuttgart.)

Contents

Introduction 6

THE LAST VOYAGE OF THE TEK SING 10
Departure 13
Captain Pearl 45
Wreck and Rescue 61
Recriminations 83

THE DISCOVERY OF THE TEK SING 97

THE PORCELAIN ON THE TEK SING 127

FROM ZHENG HE TO THE OPIUM WARS 155

Glossary 171
Selected Bibliography 174
Acknowledgements 176
Further Information 176

Introduction

The Restless M *at anchor.*
(Dave Moran.)

THIS STORY STARTS with an old and rare book, *Directions for Sailing to the East Indies,* by James Horsburgh, who was the official hydrographer to the English East India Company. Since the fifteenth century men like Horsburgh have compiled such books, also called Sea Rutters or Pilots, to provide guides for mariners. These weighty and erudite volumes are full of detailed information about the promontories and islands, rocks and reefs, currents and water depths that one might expect to meet on a particular voyage. Such books are still, of course, published today for the contemporary sailor. Horsburgh's book represented the best knowledge available at the time and was drawn from the experience of hundreds of seamen, as recorded in their log books, journals and letters. Much of this experience was hard won. A reef is often first discovered only when a ship strikes on it, sometimes with fatal consequences.

In the fifth edition of Horsburgh's book, published in 1843, on page 188 of volume two there is the following brief entry:

The Belvidere Shoals: the South West end is in latitude 2 degrees 15 minutes South and bears from Gaspar Island Peak NNW half W distant about 10 miles [16km]*; they extend from thence to the Northeastward about 4 miles* [6.4km] *being composed of several coral patches, having from six to ten feet* [1.8m–3.0m] *water upon them; and a black rock above water at the North Eastern extremity … was wrecked on these shoals a large Chinese Junk, part of whose crew reached Gaspar Island, and others, who were found floating on fragments of the wreck, were saved by the laudable exertions of a country ship belonging to Calcutta.*

That was all there was. That was the starting-point for Captain Mike Hatcher's

search beneath the equatorial blue of the South China Sea for the junk's physical remains and also for my parallel search among the dusty archives of the India Office for the junk's story. Neither search was easy.

For months the opaque surface of the water gave no clue as to the wreck's location on the sea-bed, and Horsburgh had provided neither a date nor a name for helping track down the junk in the historical records. But persistence is a necessity when it comes to hunting shipwrecks and eventually our dual quest ended in a discovery which was both immensely sad and stunningly beautiful. The enormity and also the splendour of what was revealed could hardly have been guessed at from Horsburgh's original brief and laconic entry in his Sailing Directions. The *Tek Sing* has yielded not only the largest and most spectacular haul of antique porcelain ever salvaged, but its sinking also involved a tragedy of enormous proportions with a loss of life greater than that on the *Titanic.*

The story of the junk which was eventually uncovered, provides a unique insight into the turbulent state of China at the time of its loss. It is a dramatic tale encompassing both treachery and heroism, arrogance and greed, played out against a background of opium smuggling, piracy and mass emigration. The salvaged porcelain that survives is not only intrinsically beautiful, it encapsulates and commemorates a long-forgotten fragment of history.

The opium clipper Water Witch. *(19th century, National Maritime Museum, London.)*

Above: Porcelain from the Tek Sing.
(Nagel Auctions, Stuttgart.)

Right: Map showing the routes followed by
the Indiana *and the* Tek Sing, *together*
with the main place-names referred to in
the text. The place-names are those most
frequently used in early 19th century
European sources.

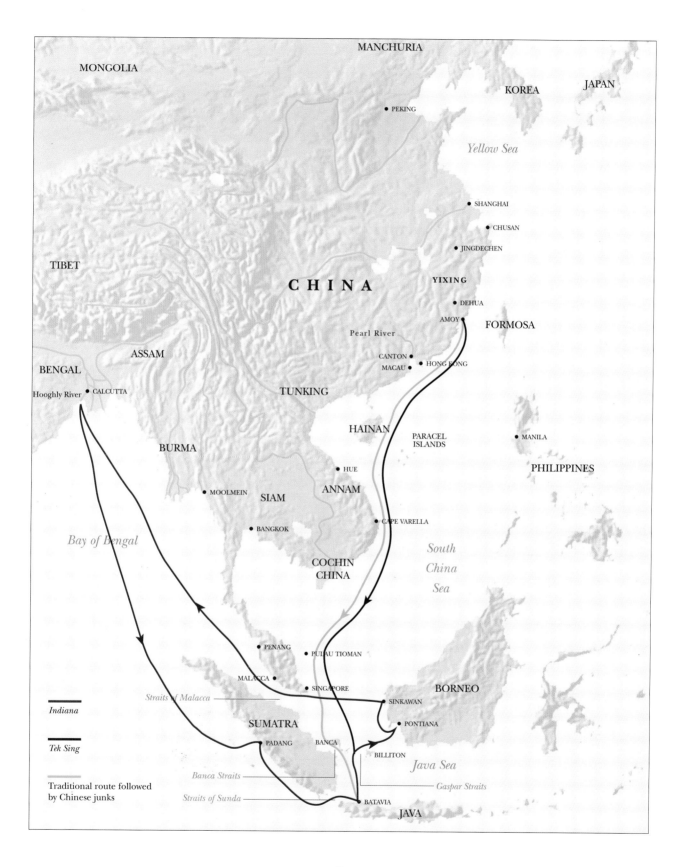

MONGOLIA

MANCHURIA

KOREA

JAPAN

TIBET

CHINA

●PEKING

Yellow Sea

●SHANGHAI

●CHUSAN

●JINGDECHEN

YIXING

●DEHUA

AMOY●

FORMOSA

ASSAM

Pearl River

CANTON●

MACAU● ●HONG KONG

BENGAL

Hooghly River ●CALCUTTA

BURMA

TUNKING

HAINAN

PARACEL
ISLANDS

●MANILA

PHILIPPINES

●HUE

●MOOLMEIN SIAM

ANNAM

●BANGKOK

●CAPE VARELLA

Bay of Bengal

COCHIN
CHINA

*South
China
Sea*

●PENANG

PULAU TIOMAN

●MALACCA ●SINGAPORE

BORNEO

Straits of Malacca

SINKAWAN

Indiana

SUMATRA

●PADANG BANCA

●PONTIANA

BILLITON

Java Sea

Tek Sing

Banca Straits

Gaspar Straits

Traditional route followed
by Chinese junks

Straits of Sunda

●BATAVIA

JAVA

9

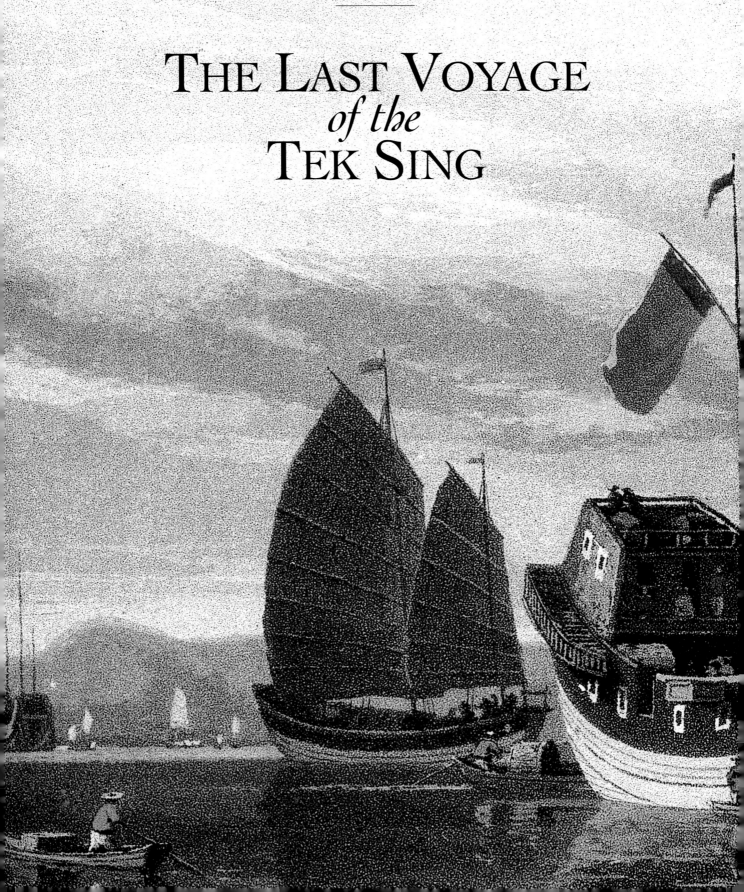

PART ONE

THE LAST VOYAGE
of the
TEK SING

Departure

AMOY, NOW KNOWN AS HSIEMEN, was (and still is) a superb natural harbour, protected on the land side by high mountains and from the sea by numerous off-lying islands. It is situated at the very hub of China's navigational routes for sailing into both the Western and the Eastern Oceans, which is how the Chinese divide up the seas that surround their coastline. The Western Ocean includes routes to Vietnam, Thailand, Borneo, India and Java. The Eastern Ocean encompasses the Philippines, Korea and Japan. Amoy, as the focal point for both East and West, has been one of China's foremost ports for more than a thousand years.

In early January 1822 a large ocean-going junk, fat bellied, with squared-off bows and stern rising high out of the water, was lying calmly at anchor in Amoy harbour. On the stern was painted an iridescently coloured, long-necked bird within an elaborate tracery of foliage. At the prow end were depicted the two huge, ever-watchful *oculi* that all sea-going junks were adorned with – staring eyes constantly scanning the horizon for any signs of danger, part of a grotesque visage designed to frighten off sea demons. The bows were painted green, which signified that the junk belonged to the port of Amoy, and they also carried the junk's identifying registration in bold red characters.

China was a highly bureaucratised country and no

Previous pages: Chinese ocean-going junks in the Pearl River estuary. A red hull signified a junk from Canton while green denoted Amoy. (National Maritime Museum, London.)

Left: A three-masted Fukien ocean-going junk with a typical high poop and a large rudder, with perforations, in the raised position. (Chinese artist, early 19th century, Martyn Gregory Gallery, London.)

aspect of life was more regulated than that pertaining to shipping and trade. Apart from the numerous taxes and duties on every conceivable item of merchandise, the Manchu regime had always been anxious about the contacts their subjects had with foreigners, because of the threat foreigners might present to internal stability. For this reason the authorities took great pains to control and limit those contacts. There were no European ships to be seen in Amoy in 1822 because Amoy, at that time, was banned to the bulk of European shipping. Only the Spanish were allowed entry, but they no longer came. At one time there had been a flourishing trade between Amoy and Manila, and Spanish ships would come on to China, having first crossed the Pacific from Acapulco. But that trade had fallen off and what ships still traversed the Amoy–Manila route were all Chinese junks. Westerners were now all confined to one place: the anchorage at Canton (Guangzhou) some five hundred kilometres or so further down the coast.

The junk's name was *Tek Sing*, which means True Star, and its destination was Batavia (now called Jakarta), the most important town on the island of Java (Jawa). Junks had been sailing this route for hundreds of years. But of late the junk trade to Batavia had also been dwindling, because more and more European and American

View of Amoy harbour. (Thomas Allom, early 19th century, University Library, Cambridge.)

Left: The gateway of Amoy during the Lantern Festival. The departure of the Tek Sing *would have involved a scene much like the one depicted here. (Auguste Borget, 1845, Martyn Gregory Gallery, London.)*

15

This painting shows chests of porcelain, for export, being transported from their place of manufacture, on the first stage of their journey overseas. (Chinese artist, late 18th century, Martyn Gregory Gallery, London.)

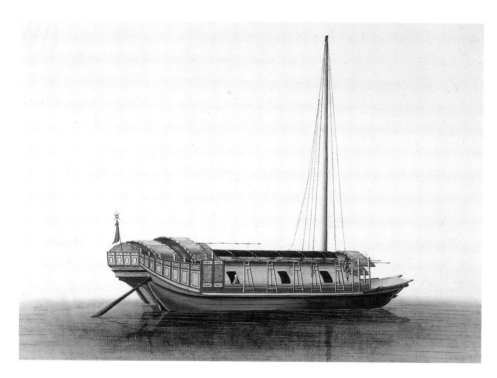

Left: Large sampans, like the one depicted here, would have been used to ferry cargo from the wharfs of Amoy to the holds of the Tek Sing. *(Captain J.H. Drummond, early 19th century, National Maritime Museum, London.)*

Below: Civil mandarin of the first rank. He is wearing a Pi Ling collar and a hat made from silk floss. The spiral of the hat is made from red coral. (Chinese artist, early 19th century, Martyn Gregory Gallery, London.)

shipping was trading directly in and out of Canton. In earlier years, four or five junks would have sailed together from Amoy to Batavia with the advent of the north-east monsoon. This year the *Tek Sing* was sailing alone. The last voyage of the *Tek Sing* represents the end of a long and great Chinese maritime tradition.

From a distance Amoy harbour was all calm and tranquillity, but on drawing closer it could be seen that this was far from the case. Small boats clustered around the sides of the great junk, like a swarm of bees around a hive, to the accompaniment of much shouting, swearing, laughter and banging of gongs. The Chinese were famous for their facility with foul language and the maritime community was particularly adept with its strings of abuse. For several days sampans had been passing busily to and fro between the quayside and the junk, loading its capacious holds with an extraordinary cornucopia of goods, both manufactured and cultivated.

At the very bottom of the holds were placed the packages of porcelain, blue and white, Swatow, celadon, *blanc de Chine*. There was porcelain for every conceivable occasion and purpose: teapots, plates, dishes, cups, cosmetic jars, ginger pots, bird feeders, water carriers, soup spoons, oil lamps, tiny figurine ornaments. This porcelain was not just the most recent production from the kilns at Jingdezhen; a large part of it consisted of special collections dating back to the seventeenth and eighteenth centuries and acquired by the connoisseur porcelain merchants of the time.

In between and on top of the porcelain was stowed the black and green teas: bohea, souchong, hyson, pekoe, twankay, gunpowder and imperial. Then came the raw silk and the nankeens. Above these were the decorative items, lacquer ware, bamboo furniture, kittysols, walking sticks, writing paper, indian inks, vermilion, cochineal, glass beads, tortoiseshell, mother-of-pearl. Boxes of incense were brought on board, sandalwood, olibanum, benjamin, myrrh. Much care was taken to stow the medicinal drugs where they would not be damaged or contaminated by seawater. Baroos camphor oil was one of the most valuable of these, obtained from trees that grew only in Sumatra (Sumatera) and Borneo (Kalimantan) between the equator and the third degree north, and not to be confused with the more common *Laurus camphora*, which could be found throughout China and Japan and which was worth only a twentieth of the price. True camphor cost more than its weight in silver. The powdered, dried roots of rhubarb were another popular drug, used as a purgative, and usually shipped in its garbled or purified form. Star anise, cassia buds, bezoar, china root, dragon's blood, ginseng and musk, all formed part of the Chinese pharmacopoeia and the *Tek Sing*'s precious cargo. Even when the holds were full there was still more cargo to be loaded. Bundles of rattans and canes, and any other items that were impervious to seawater, were strapped to the waist of the ship on the outside of the hull along the huge wooden wales that protruded about one metre wide. Not a centimetre of useful space was wasted.

The cargo on the *Tek Sing* was not intended primarily for the Western market, though it is quite probable that in the entrepôt of Batavia, some of it would be bought by Dutch, English, Swedish or French merchants eager to make up any deficiencies in the return cargoes of their own ships. The bulk of the *Tek Sing*'s goods was aimed at the wealthy Chinese community in Java itself and also the middle- and upper-class Javanese who were fond of acquiring Chinese porcelain, silks and other luxury items. Also, the cargo was not owned by a single great trading house, as was usually the way on European ships at this

Right: Sampans ferrying cargo to a junk, anchored off the China coast, on a misty morning. (George Chinnery, early 19th century, Martyn Gregory Gallery, London.)

The walled garden of a wealthy Chinese merchant. (Chinese artist, early 19th century, Martyn Gregory Gallery, London.)

Right: Chinese Hong merchants were responsible for the good conduct of the Europeans with whom they traded. The blue button on the crest of his hat indicates that he was a civil official of the fourth grade. (George Chinnery, early 19th century, Martyn Gregory Gallery, London.)

time, but by a hundred or more individual merchants. The structure of the junk reflected this ownership pattern. The *Tek Sing* was divided into about fifteen separate watertight compartments by means of transverse bulkheads. It is interesting to note that this use of watertight bulkheads had been common practice in Chinese junks since at least the fourteenth century, but was only adopted by Western shipbuilders, as a useful aid to buoyancy in the event of the ship being damaged, in the latter half of the nineteenth century. The junk's hold was also further subdivided longitud-inally, and each merchant was allotted his own section for which he was responsible. The Chinese merchants either travelled with their goods or appointed a trusted member of their family to do so on their behalf.

The quantity and richness of the cargo that was ferried out to the *Tek Sing* give little indication that by the year 1822 the Chinese economy was in severe recession. Few of the merchants busily checking their manifests can have realised that this was to be one of the last glorious voyages of a long and proud tradition. Within two decades China was to be humiliated in the first of the so-called 'Opium Wars' and

20

劉東生

Amoy would be thrown open to Western shipping as a 'treaty port'. Soon after this catastrophe, the great ocean-going junks such as the *Tek Sing* all but disappeared from the seas.

However, there was one item of the *Tek Sing*'s cargo that *did* give a clear indication that all was not well on the Chinese mainland. This was the human cargo. As well as merchants and sailors, the junk was to carry some 1,600 men, women and children aged between 6 and 70. This would have brought the total number of people on board to almost 2,000. The *Tek Sing* was a big ship – one of the very biggest of its kind, with a gross burthen of well over a thousand tonnes – but even so, with nearly two thousand people on board, conditions must have been horrendously overcrowded for all those who could not afford the luxury of a cabin.

Most of the 1,600 passengers were poor emigrants or coolies hoping to find work on the sugar plantations of Java. Indeed, it is difficult to think of them as passengers at all, because the word implies a level of comfort that must have been entirely absent. They had only the space of a rolled bamboo mat to sleep on and stow their scant possessions. They had to bring their own food supplies to last them the month that the voyage was anticipated to take. Their diet consisted entirely of rice that they boiled in pans on the deck in a random and *ad hoc* manner. There was no system of communal cooking except for the more important merchants and the sailors.

These emigrants were not regarded in a positive light by the Chinese authorities or Chinese society at large. Traditional Confucian thinking condemned a man for going abroad because it was not consistent with filial piety, which was the overriding virtue. Economic necessity, however, meant that large numbers of Chinese were prepared to ignore the stigma attached to emigration and go abroad anyway. Many were in fact little better off than bonded labourers. Some of them did not even possess enough money to pay for their voyage and would have had to remain on board ship as virtual prisoners until their liberty was purchased by a mill owner or some other would-be employer.

For hundreds of years the population of the province of Fukien (Fujian) had been in the habit of emigrating overseas during times of famine and unrest. They were a people long known for their mercantile skills and their resourcefulness. The *Indo Chinese Gleaner* of 1820 describes the people of 'Fokeen' as being 'Inwardly sincere and of a gay exterior, very attentive to business and value economy'. But the enormous numbers on board the *Tek Sing* were indicative of an unprecedented and growing crisis in Chinese society. The level of imports of opium into China had reached such proportions that the entire Chinese economy was being turned upside-down. China traditionally had had a healthy balance-of-payments surplus. Up until the beginning of the nineteenth century the rest of the world's demand for Chinese goods had always far exceeded China's own need for imports. As the Emperor Chien Lung haughtily remarked to the British ambassador Lord Macartney in 1793, 'As

your ambassador can see for himself we possess all things. I set no value on strange objects and ingenious, and have no use for your country's manufactures.' However, by 1822 the explosion in the opium trade had changed all that. Silver was draining out of China to fund its rapidly growing drug habit at such a catastrophic rate it was causing widespread economic distress.

In Fukien province, the deteriorating economic situation was made more volatile by the latent political dissidence among certain strands of society there. There were those in the southern coastal region who had never fully accepted the take-over of the Imperial throne by the Manchu dynasty in 1644. They were still loyal to the old Ming emperors, and as a symbol of that loyalty they continued to wear their hair in a tuft at the top of the head rather than adopt the Manchu shaved head and pigtail style. The Chinese community in Java was a great centre for the old Ming traditions. In the early years of the nineteenth century there was also a significant growth in clandestine movements, such as the White Lotus sects and the Triads, leading to destabilising uprisings. Many of those travelling on the *Tek Sing* would have had connections with these movements.

In the minds of the Manchu authorities emigration was a recourse for criminal types wishing to escape the hand of the law. Still worse, communities of Chinese overseas provided a breeding-ground for enemies of the state. In view of this attitude it was hardly surprising that emigration in China was, like opium smoking, strictly illegal. However, the administration was also aware that emigration could provide a

Royal palace with courtiers greeting each other and musicians playing. (Chinese artist, late 18th century, Martyn Gregory Gallery, London.)

Overleaf: The Factories, *or places of business, of the European merchants trading at Canton, flying their national flags; from left to right: Danish, French, Austrian, Swedish, British and Dutch. The foreigners were confined to this area of the city only. (Chinese artist, late 18th century, Martyn Gregory Gallery, London.)*

23

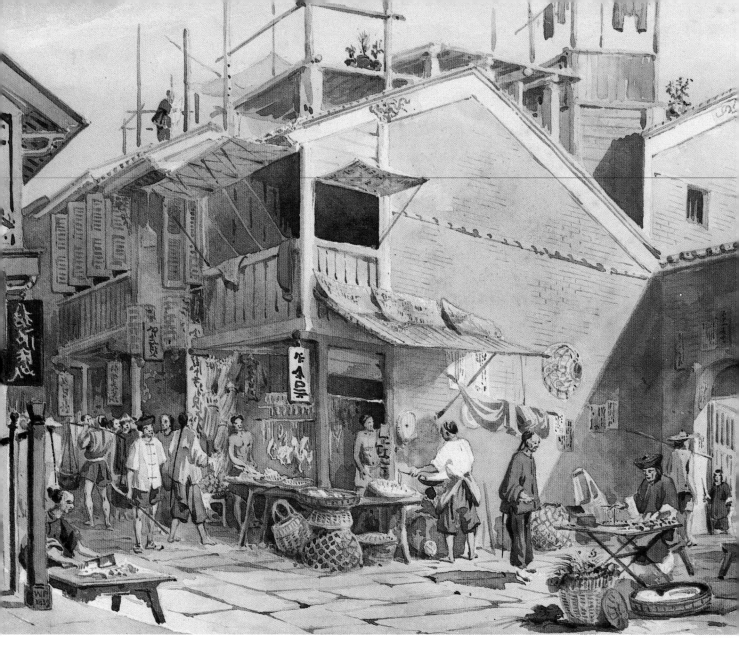

Typical Chinese street scene. (William Prinsep, 1839, Martyn Gregory Gallery, London.)

useful safety-valve in times of economic stress. Chinese labourers were in strong demand overseas. The correspondence between Rear-Admiral Henry Blackwood, situated in Trincomale, Ceylon (Sri Lanka), and J.B. Urmston at the British Factory in Canton, usefully encapsulates the realities of the situation. Blackwood wrote to Urmston early in 1822 describing Chinese workers as 'sober and industrious' and asking 'upon what terms 300 men would be likely to emigrate?' Blackwood was urgently in need of more reliable labourers than he could procure in Ceylon itself. Urmston politely wrote back in a letter dated 29 September 1822:

> *The Admiral was probably not aware that the emigration of the subjects of this Empire, is positively interdicted by the laws of the country and I have the honour of enclosing a copy of the translation of a Chinese edict which was published on this subject in the year 1815. It is true considerable numbers of Chinese are continually emigrating to Batavia, the Eastern Archipelago and Prince of Wales Island [Pinang] and adjacent places, but each emigration is at all times*

Chinese tradesmen, like this barber, would conduct their business in the street. (Thomas & William Daniell, 1810, National Maritime Museum, London.)

clandestinely done, and it would appear to be the general policy of the Chinese Government not to recognise the emigration of its subjects, so long as it is not brought publicly or officially to its notice.

Urmston goes on to suggest that the Admiral obtain his Chinese labourers through 'the principal Chinese at the Prince of Wales Island who are in the habit of acting as agents'. In other words, the procuring of emigrants was something that the Honourable English East India Company could not be seen to be dirtying its hands with, but there were Chinese middlemen who could arrange everything. Opium smuggling into China was managed in exactly the same manner.

The streets of Amoy were narrow, crowded and more than a little fetid. They were paved with large slabs of stone, beneath which the city's sewers ran. Half-centimetre gaps were left between slabs to prevent the build-up of noxious gases and make it easier to sweep away refuse. Unlike on European streets of the time, there were no horses or carriages to be seen. Everything was carried suspended from bamboo poles across the shoulder or in wheelbarrows. Wealthy mandarins or merchants were

Porcelain mender. (William Alexander, c. 1800, University Library, Cambridge.)

During the eighteenth century tea became China's most valuable export to the West. The sign on the left reads: Maolong Tea Shop. *(Chinese artist, c. 1830, Martyn Gregory Gallery, London.)*

hurried past in sedan-chairs borne along by two muscular porters. There were numerous shops, most of them open-fronted onto the street, selling every conceivable kind of product, from boots to hair-pieces, spectacles to opium pipes. The selling of tobacco or opium pipes was an offence punishable by banishment to the northern frontier to serve as a foot-soldier, but this did little to deter the offenders. Many of the shops were also places of manufacture. They had brightly painted signs hanging outside, although the signs did not signify the nature of the trade, rather some lofty slogan along the lines of 'The Harmony of right principles' or 'Trade revolves like a wheel'. Dentists and barbers attended to their clients' needs in full view of the passers-by. Every few metres there was a place selling tea and sweet confections. Cooking at the numerous cafés was done out front in the street like everything else. It was a noisy, intimate, intensely communal world. On 14 January 1822 the streets were particularly crowded and noisy, because it was the day that the *Tek Sing* was finally due to set sail. The cargo was loaded, the wind was blowing from the right quarter, and the omens were auspicious. The sailing of a sea-going junk was

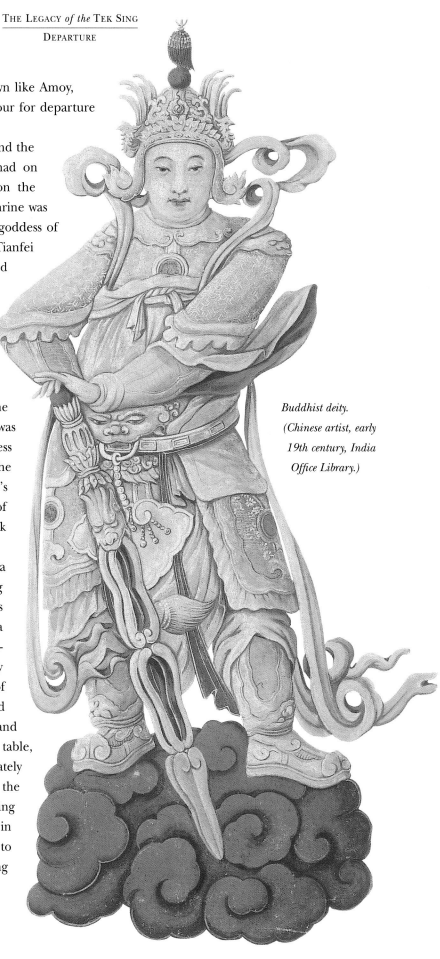

always a major occasion in the life of a town like Amoy, and the tempo of life accelerated as the hour for departure approached.

Sailors of all nations were superstitious and the Chinese were no exception. Every junk had on board its own religious shrine, situated on the poop deck close to the helm. Within the shrine was kept the ship's deity, a small statue of the goddess of the sea, Ma-tsoo po, also known as Tianfei. Tianfei was the daughter of a Fukien fisherman called Lin, who had lived towards the close of the tenth century. When she was still a girl, she had gazed into a well and been endowed with a special power to foresee the future. She warned her brother of danger when he was at sea and so enabled him to avoid drowning. After she died, a virgin, at the age of 27, her spirit was believed to roam the waves in a red dress giving assistance to distressed sailors. The sailors tied pieces of red cloth to the ship's rudder and anchor cables in memory of Tianfei's dress and to bring them good luck and a safe voyage.

The shrine was tended by a heang-kung, a priest, who kept incense sticks burning before the goddess day and night. This was partly a religious observance but also partly a very practical way of keeping time. Each joss-stick burned for 2.4 hours, the Chinese day being divided into ten parts. The image of the goddess was carved in a cross-legged sitting position out of camphor wood and painted gold and red. It was situated on a table, also painted gold and red, and also elaborately carved from camphor wood. In front of the goddess was placed a piece of wood belonging to a part of the ship, emblematic of the way in which the entire ship was being entrusted to her care. Small earthenware pots containing

Buddhist deity.
(Chinese artist, early
19th century, India
Office Library.)

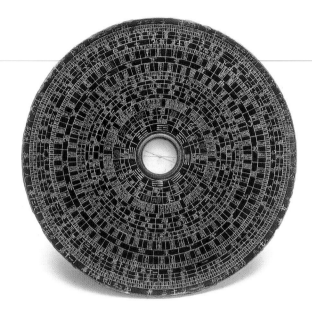

English compass made by William Farmer c. 1750 (on the left), compared with a Chinese compass of 1850. (National Maritime Museum, London.)

sacred Chinese earth and rice, symbols of the beloved homeland that was being left behind, were positioned to either side of the deity. During the voyage it was also a common practice for a pipe with tobacco to be left in the shrine, so that a sailor might enjoy a relaxing smoke while performing his devotional duties. Tobacco smoking was commonly regarded as medically beneficial, even though the authorities frowned on it.

The shrine also doubled as a compass house, the Chinese compass being another item in the sailor's pantheon of revered objects. The Chinese are generally credited with having invented the compass in around the tenth century and by the beginning of the nineteenth century its development in China had not greatly advanced. It was still just a small magnetised needle, about five centimetres long, floating on water, whereas on Western ships it was a rather more substantial affair. The main conceptual difference between the European compass and the Chinese compass, however, was that the former was divided into 32 points whereas the Chinese had 24. The Chinese also thought of the needle as pointing to the South and the Europeans to the North, though this, of course, was of no practical importance.

The evening before the *Tek Sing* was due to sail, the image of the goddess was placed on a silk cushion and conveyed with much ceremony to one of the many temples, or 'joss' houses as they were called – a term derived from 'Dios', the Portuguese for God. There the wooden goddess was presented with offerings of cooked meats, fruits and sticky rice cakes, and prayers were said imploring the deities to safeguard the voyagers on their forthcoming journey. After the prayers were finished, the offerings of food and drink that the gods had not consumed were gratefully received by all those who had taken part in the ceremony. And then the festivities began. Everywhere on the streets there were small troupes of actors, jugglers, acrobats and musicians. Outside the temple, the square was lined with hundreds of little stalls selling cakes, caps, purses, trinkets, combs, jewellery and all manner of adornments and knick-knacks. The noise from gongs, tom-toms, pipes and horns was deafening. And above all the racket there were the continual explosions of firecrackers. Coloured paper lanterns, in the shapes of fish, lions and mythological dragons, suspended from long poles, swung back and forth in the night air. And slowly the procession for departure wound its way through the town and passed out beneath the great stone gate of Amoy, appropriately surmounted by two large sculptures of fish and quotations from Confucius. The crowds were huge. Not only were there the two thousand people who were about to set sail for Batavia, but there were all their friends and family who had come to see them off, together with all those revellers who had just joined in for a good time.

Street entertainer. (Chinese artist, c. 1800, Martyn Gregory Gallery, London.)

The captain of the *Tek Sing* was called Io Tauko. He was a very experienced seaman, having made the annual voyage to Batavia for at least the five previous years, always in the same ship. Ownership of the ship and its cargo was divided among the members of an entire guild, but Io Tauko was the head man and co-ordinator and the person who made the final decisions, particularly those relating to trade. His status was roughly equivalent to the supercargo on board a Western ship of the time.

As the tide lifted on the morning of 14 January, the order was given for the heavy wooden anchors to be raised. It was probably not Io Tauko who gave this order, although he was almost certainly on deck at the time. All matters relating to navigation were left to the hochang, or ship's pilot. The next most important man on board, below the hochang, was the to-kung, or helmsman, who was responsible for the rudder and the sails. The sailors were divided into two main classes: the tow-muh, who possessed specific skills relating to some part of the ship; and the ho-ke, who carried out the more unskilled menial work such as hauling on ropes.

Sailors on board a Chinese junk had a very different status from sailors on board a Western ship of the time. They were not paid wages, but were all small-time merchants in their own right, being allocated a quota of cargo space in exchange for their labour. The German missionary Gutzlaff, who travelled on an ocean-going junk in 1832, and who was not averse to a little opium trading in the cause of spreading Christianity, recorded his impressions of the crew in the following unflattering terms:

These sailors are not, usually, men who have been trained up to their occupation, but wretches who were obliged to flee from their homes; and they frequently engage for a voyage before they have ever been on board a junk. All of them, however stupid, are commanders; and if anything of importance is to be done, they will bawl out their commands to each other, till all is utter confusion. There is no subordination, no cleanliness, no mutual regard or interest.

One has to place these observations in the context of Western Protestant prejudice, but it is evident from Gutzlaff, and from other commentators, that the relationship between crew and captain on a Chinese junk was more informal, and in a way more democratic, than it was on, say, an East Indiaman of the period.

Once the anchors were raised, the order was given to hoist the huge bamboo and matting sails. These were so heavy that they took almost two hours to get into position, but they had the advantage of being easy and quick to furl in times of severe weather, without the need for men to go aloft into the rigging and risk falling into the sea. The *Tek Sing* had three masts. In the days of Zheng He, in the fifteenth century, sea-going junks had been constructed with up to nine masts. But the number of masts allowed on sea-going junks was now limited to three by Imperial decree, in an attempt to curtail their size and speed, and also, therefore, their usefulness as potential warships. The ruling Manchu regime was always concerned about the possibility of rebellion or piracy by its sea-going subjects. But like so many Chinese regulations this one was of little practical significance. The *Tek Sing* was quite large enough and fast enough to be equipped as a formidable warship, should its owners have chosen to do so.

The wind filled the huge matting sails and the *Tek Sing* edged its way southwards down the channel of water between the mainland and the beautiful island of Ku-Lang-Yu, circled with beaches of golden sand. This island was to become a favourite place of residence for wealthy colonials when the port of Amoy was finally opened up to Europeans after China's defeat in the Opium Wars. The final departure of the *Tek Sing* was accompanied by more frenzied beating of gongs and tom-toms. Gilt paper was scattered on the waves for good luck. The decks were crowded with people, not just so they could shout last farewells to family and friends, but because that was the only available space. Most of the emigrants would be living, cooking and sleeping on two metres of open planking for the next month. The merchants had cabins at the poop end of the ship, ramshackle thatched creations built one on top of the other in a kind of crazy multi-storey tower. They were rented out by the sailors, who would themselves occupy them if they could not be gainfully let. The captain and the more important merchants inhabited more spacious accommodation on the main deck, also at the stern end of the ship. For the rest, it was a matter of whatever

Right: The Prussian Gutzlaff in oriental costume. He combined missionary work with opium peddling and spying for the British. (Early 19th century, Hulton Getty Picture Collection.)

Gedr. v. A. Kneisel, Leipzig

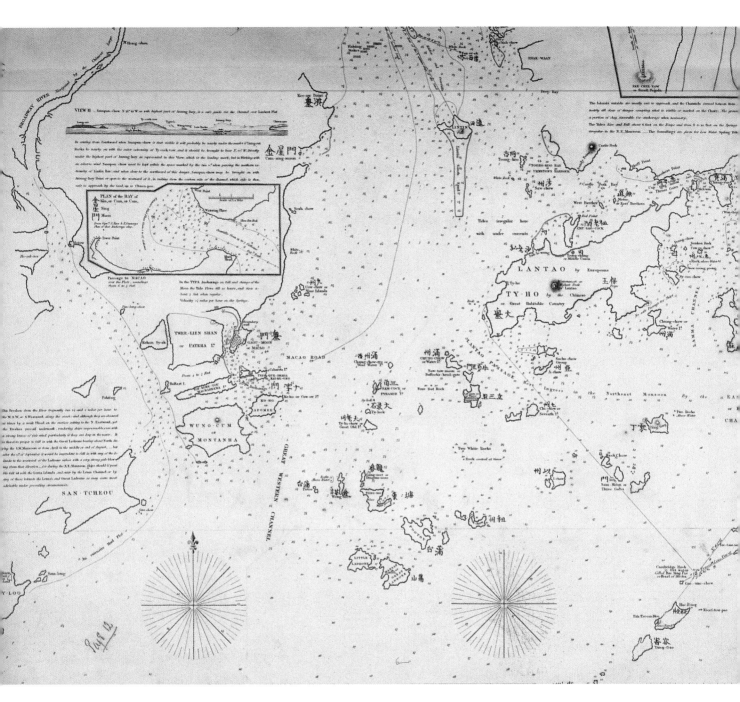

Detail from a chart of the Canton River, also known as the Pearl River. (1831, University Library, Cambridge.)

nook or cranny they could find to crawl into. As the *Tek Sing* headed towards the open sea, those that looked back could see the tombs of their ancestors on the hills above Amoy.

For several hours after the *Tek Sing* had started on its southerly journey, small boats continued to ferry backwards and forwards. They carried last-minute passengers, important letters, fresh produce, prostitutes, and almost certainly a wide array of smuggled goods. During the next day or so, crew and passengers settled down to the usual shipboard routine. The *Tek Sing* ran before the wind in a south-westerly direction. When the weather was fine the dramatic mountains of the Fukien coast, where the famous bohea teas were grown, were clearly visible on the starboard side, a reassuring sight to those who had never been to sea before. The sailors, when they weren't pulling on the huge hawsers that worked the rudder and the sails, spent their time gambling, swearing, drinking arrack and smoking opium. Chinese sailors were notoriously addicted to gambling, dice being a favourite pastime, together with quail fighting and a simple game which involved guessing accurately the number of fingers raised simultaneously by both oneself and one's opponent. It is unlikely that the *Tek Sing* carried a cargo of opium in its holds, because Batavia received most of its supplies direct from Bengal in European ships, but it is inconceivable that opium was not widely smoked on board, by both emigrants and sailors. And no doubt some of the richer merchants carried their own personal jars of the refined drug for use in their cabins.

Once out in the open sea, the ship progressed at a good rate of about 5 knots an hour, covering about 130 nautical miles a day, or 10 keng. To make this kind of progress it was necessary to sail through the night rather than anchor up, but night-time sailing was the customary practice. This part of the route was well known and the hazards were familiar ones. Regular soundings were taken, using a lead weight on a length of rope made from bamboo fibre, to keep a check on the depth of water the ship was in. Sailors did not fear deep water. Shoal water was the danger. They also measured the progress of the ship by dropping a line in the sea at the bow of the ship and walking with it to the stern and then hauling it out again. The length of the line that had been paid out, less the length of the ship, was the distance travelled during the time it had taken to walk from the front of the ship to the stern. The pilot would constantly take samples from the sea-bed. The different kinds of sandy or muddy bottom provided further clues as to where they were. During the daytime there were landmarks on the coastline to observe because Chinese junks rarely ventured out of sight of the coast unless it was absolutely unavoidable. And at night there were the stars to navigate by.

The *Tek Sing* ran past Pedra Branca (Zhenyantou), an enormous pillar of white rock sticking straight up from the sea. A little further on, the blue waters changed to a muddier, darker colour where the giant Pearl River (Zhu Jiang) disgorged into the sea. In the distance could be seen Lintin Island, a notorious place for opium smuggling. It was most probably in the vicinity of Lintin that the *Tek Sing* fell in with another, smaller junk, called a wangkang, that was to play an important part in the events that followed. The wangkang was captained by a man called Tjieuw Kingliang. It had a red bow with blue lettering, which signified that it came from Canton. Like the *Tek Sing* it had emigrants on board, but only 198 as opposed to the *Tek Sing*'s

This view of the Boca Tigris, at the entrance to the Pearl River, shows a Chinese ocean-going junk in the foreground, with a fast customs boat to the left of it, and a British merchant ship to the right. The Boca Tigris had forts on both sides which were designed to guard the entrance to Canton. (Chinese artist, early 19th century, Martyn Gregory Gallery, London.)

1,600. The two captains no doubt exchanged the latest news. Tjieuw Kingliang would have told Io Tauko of the dramatic events that had recently taken place in Canton.

A Sicilian sailor called Francis Terranovia, who belonged to an American ship called the *Emily*, had been bargaining with a Chinese woman on a sampan about the price of the fruit she was selling. In a fit of rage the sailor had thrown an olive jar at the woman, which knocked her on the head and killed her. The Chinese authorities demanded the sailor should be put on trial. The American captain refused to hand his crew member over. The authorities then followed the usual procedure of arresting and throwing into prison the luckless Chinese 'security merchant' who was responsible for the *Emily*, a man called Pacqua. The entire Canton trade was brought to a halt because of the incident. Eventually Terranovia was transferred into the custody of the Chinese, put on trial and executed. But this was far from being the end of the affair. It transpired that the *Emily*, like most independent American and British ships trading into Canton at the time, had been smuggling opium. There was an enormous public furore over the case. On 6 November 1821, one of the most important and wealthiest of the Chinese merchants in Canton, called Howqua, was charged with participating in the opium trade, and the Canton Governor Yuen Tajin deprived him of his symbolic button, as a mark of his disgrace. Yuen Tajin then wrote to the European merchants on 2 December 1821 in the following outraged terms:

The Celestial Empire permits tea, rhubarb etc to be sold to keep alive the people of the said Nations, those persons who are annually kept alive thereby, are more than ten thousand times ten thousand. How substantial a favour is this! Yet these foreigners feel no gratitude, nor wish to render a recompense, but smuggle in prohibited opium, which flows, and poisons the land.

The scandal came to encompass other ships and other traders. James Matheson, of the famous company Jardine Matheson, was forced to withdraw two of his ships, the *Hooghly* and the *Merope*. The *Merope* had carried 700 chests of best Bengal opium. They left the Pearl River and anchored off Lintin Island in order to continue their trading activities outside the control of the Chinese authorities. They were still anchored there when the *Tek Sing* sailed past. The opium crisis meanwhile continued

A Chinese trial of British seamen at a court in Canton. The merchant Howqua is depicted on the left, with the leading British merchants opposite him. (Chinese artist, early 19th century, National Maritime Museum, London.)

to deepen, and on 10 January 1822, the same day that the wangkang left Canton, the East India Company also withdrew all their ships, personnel and treasure from the Pearl River and anchored off Lintin. The East India Company ships did not officially carry opium, but they were worried that they might get caught up in the general purge on foreigners, and their officials also be thrown into jail and their property confiscated.

Captain Tjieuw Kingliang would, no doubt, have been full of this exciting gossip when he met up with Io Tauko in the *Tek Sing*. From this point on the two ships sailed in company. There was some comfort to be had from having a consort, particularly in the pirate-infested waters that their voyage took them through. One of the main

Left: This painting shows an opium-smuggling ship at Capsing-Moon Passage. (Artist unknown, c. 1840, National Maritime Museum, London.)

Above: Portrait of Benjamin Smith, an American sea-captain. (The Chinese artist known as Spoilum, c. 1800, Martyn Gregory Gallery, London.)

differences between Chinese junks and Western ships was that the former carried far fewer armaments. This was because the quantity of armaments allowed on a junk was strictly regulated by Imperial edict. A ship like the *Tek Sing* was only allowed two cannon, eight smaller musket-style guns called gingalls, ten swords, ten sets of bows and arrows and about eighteen kilograms of gunpowder. The reason for this strict limitation was once again fear on the part of the Chinese authorities that if a junk were allowed to carry a heavier armament, its captain might be tempted to turn pirate. The corollary of this, however, was that junks were far more susceptible to piracy than the heavily armed Western ships.

After passing Lintin Island, the two junks continued to sail along the Kwangtung

coast in a south-westerly direction, eventually turning onto a more southerly tack to pass along the east side of Hainan. From there they navigated between the notorious Paracel Islands, scene of countless shipwrecks, and the Vietnam coast, then known as Cochin China, being careful to keep the Paracels well to the port. They left the Cochin coast behind at Cape Varella (Mui Varella), where there was an important shrine to the goddess Tianfei. Passing Chinese sailors always made an offering to the goddess at this point of the voyage. They constructed a small model boat a little over a metre in length, fitted it out with all the accoutrements of a real sailing-ship, including toy rudder, sails, cannon and miniature people, victualled it with food and water and cast it on the sea. This ritual took place to the accompaniment of the usual gongs, the burning of incense and the showering of glittery paper on the waves. Afterwards there was a feast of cooked pork and sweet cakes, though few if any of the emigrants could have partaken of such luxuries.

Cape Varella was an important point of departure, because from here the junks lost sight of the coast and headed across the open sea towards the Malay Peninsula

Left: Portrait of Howqua, one of the most astute of the Chinese Hong merchants. Despite losing his button of office over the Emily *incident, he still managed to die a wealthy man. (Chinese artist, early 19th century, Martyn Gregory Gallery, London.)*

Below: This Chinese pirate flag is supposed to depict Tianfei, the goddess of the sea. (Chinese artist, c. 1800, National Maritime Museum, London.)

and Pulau Tioman. After a landfall had been made on
Tioman Island the usual route would have carried
them along the east coast of the Malay Peninsula, past
Seven Islands, through the Banca Straits (Selat
Bangka), and finally along the coast of Sumatra to
Batavia. However, somewhere in the vicinity of Tioman,
Io Tauko made a fateful decision not to follow the
customary course of Chinese junks through the Banca
Straits, which had been the tried and tested route for
many centuries past, but to stay out in mid-ocean and
head for the Gaspar Straits (Selat Gelasa) between
Billiton (Belitung) and the east side of Banca Island.
We will never know exactly what his thinking was that
led him to this decision. It is possible he decided to
avoid the Banca Straits because of the increased
depredations by pirates in this narrow passage in
recent years. Alternatively, he may have decided that
the Gaspar Straits simply offered a quicker passage.
These Straits had been explored by a number of
European ships during the previous thirty years and
were widely talked of as providing a safer, faster route
between China and the southern archipelago. With so
many people on board, many of whom would probably
by this stage have been hungry and ill disciplined, and
also the likelihood of fresh-water shortages, Io Tauko
may well have decided that the shorter route offered
valuable advantages. Certainly Tjieuw Kingliang
disclaimed any responsibility for the decision. He
afterwards stated that he was at all times following
behind the *Tek Sing*. But the waters of this route were
still far from being thoroughly charted. Whatever the
explanation, the decision was a disastrous one.

*The coast of Cochin China, near Cape Varella, where the crews of
passing Chinese junks customarily paid homage to Tianfei. (Thomas
& William Daniell, c. 1810, University Library, Cambridge.)*

Captain Pearl

IN LATE DECEMBER OF 1821, the Hooghly (Hugli) River
which flows through the city of Calcutta in Bengal,
India, was choked with shipping. There were Arab
dhows, Chinese junks, Indian budgerows, American
and European traders, the private pleasure boats of
wealthy baboos, and darting between all these various
craft, the tiny canoes of the river beggars. Moored close
to Chandpaul Ghaut, the main wharf at the very centre
of Calcutta's busy river frontage, was a fine new English
'country' ship called the *Indiana*. The larger East
Indiamen could not get upriver as far as Calcutta. They
had to unload at Diamond Harbour, some sixty
kilometres nearer the sea, and transfer passengers and
cargo to barges and budgerows. The very biggest ships
could get no further than Kedgeree, another fifty
kilometres below Diamond Harbour. One of the
advantages of country ships was that they were of
sufficiently shallow draught to be able to moor right
opposite the wharfs and quays of Calcutta itself.

The *Indiana*, 374 tonnes, had been built in Calcutta
shipyards in 1818 from the finest teak, and the hull had
been sheathed with copper both to increase speed and
to protect it from worm. In appearance it had much in
common with the streamlined opium clippers that
were developed a few years later and which were
specially designed to beat against the wind up the
South China Sea. Standing on the deck was James

*Left: A view of Calcutta from
a point opposite Kidderpore,
with Indian fishing vessels
and coconut palms in the
foreground. (James Fraser,
1819, University Library,
Cambridge.)*

Country vessels at anchor on the Hooghly River. These vessels were privately owned by both Indian and European merchants and traded exclusively within the Asian region. (Franz Solvyns, 1792, National Maritime Museum, London.)

Pearl, captain of the *Indiana* and also its proud new owner. Pearl had seen service in the Royal Navy as a lieutenant during the Napoleonic Wars. At the end of those wars in 1815, he found himself, like many another British officer who had served in the forces, without an obvious career. Being of an adventurous nature, he decided to seek his fortune in the Orient. According to the *Bengal Directory*, he first arrived in India in 1817 and shortly after that he was appointed captain of the *Indiana*, then owned by the powerful trading house of Barretto & Sons who had establishments in Calcutta and Macao. Captain Pearl's fortunes prospered and within a few years he had bought the *Indiana* from Barretto and was trading on his own behalf. He was what was called in the general parlance 'a country trader', that is a European shipowner whose arena of activities was confined to inter-island trading in the eastern archipelago, including India and China, rather than engaging in the long-haul trade from Europe to the Far East.

It was early morning. The *Indiana* was loading cargo before the heat of the day made heavy physical work almost unendurable. Large numbers of the native population, men and women, came down to the river's edge and waded into the water up to their waists, in order to wash themselves and their garments. Calcutta at this period was expanding fast, with ambitious new road schemes and buildings. One

Budgerows were used to transport passengers on the higher reaches of the Hooghly River, where the large East Indiamen could not sail. The Union Jack indicates that the passengers on board this budgerow were British. The blinds at the stern of the vessel are drawn down against the glare of the sun. (Murshidabad artist, c. 1800, Martyn Gregory Gallery, London.)

Chandpaul Ghaut was the main landing-place for Europeans first arriving in Calcutta. Large numbers of native Indians also used it as a bathing area. (James Fraser, 1819, University Library, Cambridge.)

of the most impressive of these was Government House on Esplanade Row. It had been constructed by Lord Wellesley when he was Governor-General in 1802. He had announced that he wished 'India to be ruled from a palace not a counting house'. Government House was indeed a palace of massive proportions, approached by a gracious carriage drive, adorned with circular colonnades and grand porticoes, proudly bearing the coat of arms of the East India Company on each of its north wings, and crowned with a gleaming dome. It says something about the power of a Governor-General of the time, that Lord Wellesley built it without even bothering to mention what he was doing to the ruling Court of Directors of the East India Company back in England. In 1824 James Atkinson wrote a poem about Calcutta, in which he called it a 'City of Palaces'. From where Captain Pearl was standing it was an apt description. Mosques, pagodas, churches and temples all shimmered against the skyline. Writing later in the same century, Kipling described the town as the 'City of Dreadful Night'. He was referring to the poverty, the prostitution and the corrupt underbelly of colonialism. Captain Pearl knew something about that too.

Coming west down Esplanade Row which led towards the river at Chandpaul Ghaut, situated between the Town Hall and the Treasury, was the imposing façade of

A typical opium clipper. These streamlined vessels were able to sail against the wind and complete three voyages a year between India and China. The Indiana *was a forerunner of this kind of ship. (William Huggins, 1844, Martyn Gregory Gallery, London.)*

A view of Government House, Calcutta, from Court House Street. Built by Lord Wellesley in 1802, it symbolised British Imperial self-confidence. (James Fraser, 1819, University Library, Cambridge.)

the Salt and Opium Department. It was here that free traders like James Pearl bought their supplies of opium directly from the English East India Company, which had the controlling monopoly. Once purchased, the opium was ferried from the export warehouses in Takshall Street, just south of the old Fort William, to the holds of the country ships like the *Indiana*. Each crate of the drug was stamped with the coat of arms of King George IV as a seal of quality. Best Bengal opium was used throughout the East as a form of currency as universally acceptable as silver dollars.

Above: Lord Hastings was Governor-General of India in 1822. This painting, designed to celebrate his name, was positioned at the top of the staircase of the Town Hall, for a Grand Ball given on 1 December 1819. It shows the suppression of those native Indians who were rebellious, as opposed to the gratitude of those who loved peace and plenty. (George Chinnery, 1819, Martyn Gregory Gallery, London.)

The English East India Company did not permit its own ships to be used for the opium trade to China, from fear that disapproval by the Chinese authorities might lead to a disruption of its valuable tea trade. Instead, it sold the opium, while still in India, to free traders who then carried out the more risky business of onward shipment. The big profits were to be made in carrying opium from Calcutta to Canton. But to participate in what James Jardine was to call 'this most gentlemanly trade', it was necessary to have established contacts within the Chinese community at

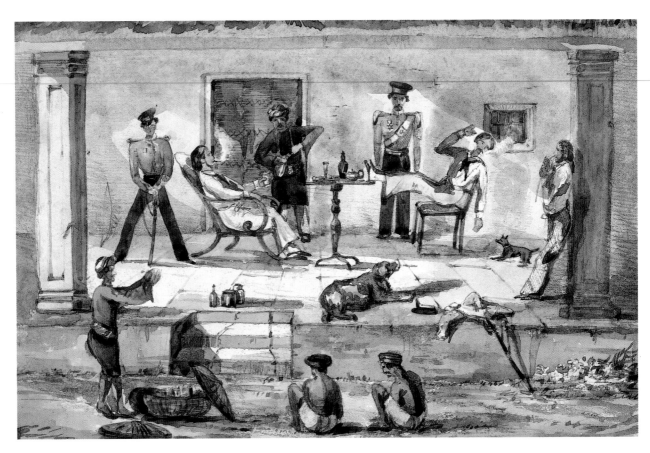

British officers in Calcutta relaxing in their living quarters, called a chummery. *(National Army Museum, London.)*

Right: Clive of India. It was his military victory at the Battle of Plassey in 1757 which established the English East India Company as an Imperial power and subsequently enabled it to monopolise and stimulate the production of opium. (Thomas Gainsborough, c. 1764, National Army Museum, London.)

the Canton end. James Pearl, as a relative newcomer to the East, was not part of this network. But there were alternative opium circuits for those prepared for a high-risk strategy, and it was one of these that he had planned.

In the December opium sales that had just taken place, James Pearl had purchased 175 chests of best Behar. He had paid something over 1,500 rupees per chest. He hoped to sell them again for well over 2,000 rupees each, and anticipated a profit on the whole voyage in excess of 100,000 rupees or 10,000 pounds sterling, enough to set a man up for life. It was, in his own words, 'a commercial voyage of great speculation'. He checked each chest carefully as it was brought onto the *Indiana*. Every crate contained forty cakes of opium that weighed about 1.3kg each. The cakes were a dark brown colour, solidified on the outside with a more viscous mixture within. In Chinese slang the substance was known as 'foreign mud' or 'black smoke'. Pearl had been careful to ensure that his opium cakes had not been adulterated somewhere down the line of production. Mixing in powdered dried opium stalks with gum arabic was a favourite trick of the crooked opium dealer. The cakes were wrapped in animal skins and covered in gunny, which was a kind of coarse jute sacking, before being put into the chests.

The *Indiana* was manned by a crew of fifty natives and four Europeans. The

Above: The opium smoker depicted here is heating his opium on an earthenware stove, very similar to the stoves found on the Tek Sing. *His pipe and pillow are already waiting on his couch. (Chinese artist, c. 1800, Martyn Gregory Gallery, London.)*

Right: Opium smoker in a high-class brothel. The bed, with its carefully folded quilts pushed to the back and elaborate hangings, is typical of the late Qing period. Positioned between the two footstools is a spitoon. (Chinese artist, early 19th century, Martyn Gregory Gallery, London.)

Europeans were the commander, the chief officer, the second officer and the third officer. Most of the seamen were Lascars. In addition the native crew would include a gunner, a carpenter, a cook, a serang, a tindal, a bhandarry, three topasses and four seacunnies. The total wages for a three-month voyage, excluding the captain, came to less than 3,000 rupees or £300. Food and drink for all might be expected to cost a further 500 rupees or £50. The entire costs for the voyage would, therefore, come to not much more than the profit that one might reasonably expect to make on the sale of half a dozen chests of opium.

It was Captain Pearl's intention to sail down the west coast of Sumatra to Padang (Teluk Bayur) and then through the Sunda Straits (Selat Sunda) to Batavia. From there, his plan was to beat up against the north-east monsoon to Sinkawan on the west coast of Borneo. The major import from Bengal, at both Padang and Batavia, was Patna and Benares opium. But both these trading-posts had the drawback that they were under Dutch control and the Dutch imposed heavy duties on opium imports. These duties creamed off most of the profit, and from Captain Pearl's own later statements on the subject, it seems unlikely that he had ever intended to sell much or any of his opium cargo at these ports. The west coast of Borneo, on the other hand, offered far more exciting opportunities to the aspiring opium dealer.

This raises the question as to why, if Borneo was his final destination, he chose to sail the Sunda Straits route, rather than the more direct route through the Malacca Straits. The only explanation is that he most probably intended to do a little trading in gunpowder, rum and cotton piece goods at Padang and Batavia, and he may also have wished to purchase some small quantities of coffee, which was available at both places. Coffee was in brisk demand back in Bengal. It is also possible that he may simply have been persuaded of the virtues of this route by the single mysterious passenger he was carrying, a Mr R. Jack, who wanted to travel to Batavia. What is very clear, from Captain Pearl's subsequent statements, is that it was Borneo, not Padang or Batavia, that provided the real lure of the trading venture that he had embarked upon.

At first glance Borneo, densely forested and difficult to penetrate, might seem an unlikely destination for an ambitious young merchant. In 1822 it was still largely unknown and unvisited by Europeans. The interior was populated mainly by Dayaks, who lived by hunting and fishing in a style that had remained relatively unchanged since the neolithic period and included such practices as cannibalism and head-shrinking, though they were generally regarded as a shy and amiable race. The Malays had populated large areas of the coast, living mainly from fishing and piracy. The Dutch had invaded in 1780 and they had established a fort at Sambas and a presence at Pontiana (Pontianak), but they had never succeeded in imposing the kind of bureaucratic and military control that they had exerted over Java for the previous two centuries. Borneo didn't pay for the Dutch. On the contrary, it was a continual drain on the resources of Batavia. By the beginning of the nineteenth century their presence on the enormous island was still very minimal, just a handful of soldiers and a couple of civilian administrators in total.

What drew Captain Pearl to the shores of Borneo was not the Dutch nor the Malays, nor the Dayaks. It was the presence of the Chinese. Trade between China and Borneo stretched back for thousands of years. Chinese vases were treated with totemic significance by the Dayaks and formed an important part of their religious ceremonies. Offers of over a thousand dollars for a single vase were known to have

LASCARI-BÂT.

A

COLLECTION OF SENTENCES USED
IN THE DAILY-ROUTINE
OF

MODERN PASSENGER STEAMERS
WHERE

LASCARS ARE CARRIED AS THE
DECK CREW;
ALSO A

COPIOUS ENGLISH-LASCARI VOCABULARY.

New and Re-Written Edition,
COMPILED BY
A. L. VALENTINI
(*Commander, Peninsular and Oriental Steam Navigation
Company's Service*).

PUBLISHED BY
MILLER & SONS, CENTRAL AVENUE, ROYAL ALBERT DOCKS,
LONDON.

Third Edition, 1901.

From the end of the eighteenth century ships like the Indiana, *as well as the larger vessels which sailed between Europe and Asia, were increasingly crewed by Indian sailors. The generic term for these sailors was* lascars *and their prevalence resulted in a number of Indian words being adopted into the English language. (A.L. Valentini, 1901, National Maritime Museum, London.)*

Captain Pearl's voyage from Padang to Batavia would have taken him through the Straits of Sunda. This painting shows the homeward-bound East India Company fleet at anchor in the Sunda Straits. (William Daniell, c. 1810, National Maritime Museum, London.)

been refused. The Chinese, in turn, took back to their own country the much-coveted birds' nests of the *Hirundo esculenta*, a kind of small swallow. These nests, found deep in caves, were about the size of a goose egg and weighed only between seven and 14 grams. The most prized nests were taken before the bird had had the time to lay any eggs, because at that stage they were still white and unfouled. If the eggs had hatched and the nests had become dirty and streaked with blood they were only worth a tenth of their unsullied value. The best nests fetched twice their weight in silver. For hundreds of years the Chinese had simply come to Borneo as traders. There had been no attempt to colonise. But at the beginning of the nineteenth century, large numbers of Chinese, disaffected with the Manchu regime, left their homeland and settled in Borneo to exploit the latter's legendary gold resources. Chinese junks began to visit Borneo on their way to Java, or as an alternative to Java, in greater numbers than before – not just to carry on their traditional trade, but also

Arab traders introduced opium into India around the third century AD and it was used for medicinal purposes long before it was cultivated as a narcotic. The Chinese physician, Chen-Heng, writing in the fourteenth century, warned: Great care must be taken in using it because it kills like a knife. *(Opium poppy, Chinese artist, early 19th century, Martyn Gregory Gallery, London.)*

to supply the growing Chinese community. The growth in the junk trade led to further possibilities: why transport valuable Chinese goods destined for onward sale to Batavia and pay the high duties imposed by the Dutch, if you could sell them free of such duties on the Borneo coast? By the same token, why pay high duties on the import of opium if you could sell that same opium free of taxes directly to a large community of Chinese consumers, and take receipts in gold dust? For a brief period around 1820, the west coast of Borneo had the possibility of developing into one of the major free trade centres of the East. Sinkawan, and some of the other small harbours, certainly became important destination points for all the buccaneers and freebooters chancing their luck in the opium business.

Opium bale with the official stamp of Queen Victoria, guaranteeing quality. (Illustrated London News Picture Library.)

As it turned out, the Dutch had other ideas, and it was the newly founded free port of Singapore that was to reap this colossal commercial harvest, while the west coast of Borneo was very rapidly to return to being an insignificant backwater. It was to be Captain Pearl's bad luck to become disastrously caught up in these fast-shifting political and commercial quicksands.

Wreck and Rescue

THE FIRST PART OF Captain Pearl's voyage went predictably enough. The *Indiana* slipped quietly down the river past the elegant country houses of the more senior members of the Indian Civil Service, such as that belonging to William Farquharson, situated at Garden Reach eight kilometres downstream from Calcutta, with gardens that stretched down to the water's edge, shaded by gracious banyan trees. Sailing out of Padang, an albatross was seen. And, entering the Sunda Straits, one of the officers harpooned a shark, which led to much jubilation among the members of the crew.

Batavia was reached on 12 January, just a day or so before the *Tek Sing* left Amoy. The American ship *Emily*, which had been at the centre of the opium-smuggling furore at Canton the previous month, had also just arrived in Batavia. The single passenger on board the *Indiana*, Mr Jack, disembarked. Nothing is known about him beyond that simple bald statement in the *Bataviasche Courant*.

The *Indiana* left Batavia again on 27 January, having taken on fresh water and supplies. The going from this point became extremely difficult. The north-east monsoon was blowing strongly against them and it was hard work to keep tacking into the wind. It took the *Indiana* ten days to cover a distance that with favourable winds it would have done in two.

Left: Passengers being rescued from a wrecked vessel in stormy seas. (Edward Bamfylde, 1805, National Maritime Museum, London.)

The Alceste *was wrecked in the Gaspar Straits in 1816 after striking a sunken reef. The survivors took refuge on Pulau Leat and watched while the stranded wreck was set on fire by pirates. One of those on board the* Alceste *was Lord Amherst, returning from an unsuccessful diplomatic mission to China. (Midshipman C.W. Browne, 1818, National Maritime Museum, London.)*

But then a less handy ship would not have been able to make any progress at all.

Close to the equator the sun usually comes up quickly and the transition from dark to light is rapid, but on the morning of 7 February first light was a much slower business than usual, owing to a dark covering of cloud, heavy rain and the squally conditions. The *Indiana* was threading its way cautiously through the treacherous reefs of the Gaspar Straits between Banca and Billiton, still two or three degrees short of the equator. The weather, despite the rain, was oppressively hot. Progress was wearyingly slow. During the night they had navigated safely between Salt Island (today called Lepar) and Middle Island, also known as Pulau Leat (today called Liat). This had taken them past the infamous Discovery Rock charted by Lieutenant Ross in HMS *Discovery* seven years earlier, in 1815. This rock lurked about a metre or more beneath the surface of the water, and had been the scene of numerous shipwrecks, both before and since Lieutenant Ross had laid it down in the charts. But other hazards still lay ahead, not least Vansittart Reef where the East India Company ship *Vansittart* had struck in 1789, with the loss of the ship and 53 chests of silver. Captain Lestock Wilson of the *Vansittart* had been carrying out one of the first hydrographic surveys of these waters ever undertaken when his ship was wrecked. One might have

62

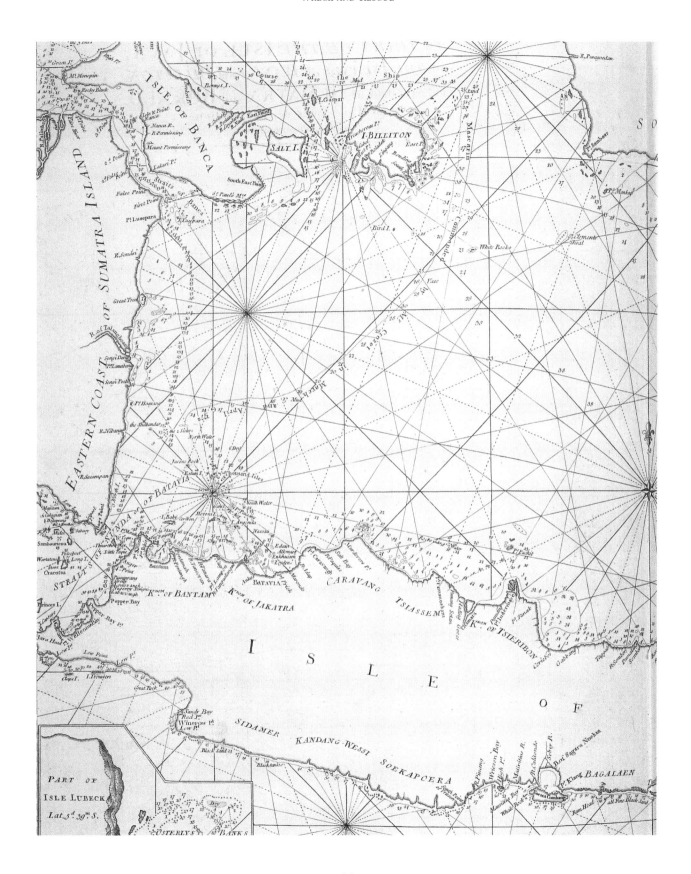

Previous page: A chart of the isle of Java, dated 1778, published by Sayer & Bennett, and based on the work of the celebrated French hydrographer M. D'Apres de Mannevillette. It does not show the Belvidere Reef, the existence of which was unknown at that date. (University Library, Cambridge.)

Guns like this one were used by landing parties in small boats. (1793, National Maritime Museum, London.)

thought that Lestock Wilson's own fate, and the subsequent losses of so much other shipping, would have resulted in this particular route to China being abandoned altogether in favour of the more traditional and better-known Banca Straits. But the shorter passage that the new route offered was an irresistible lure to traders eager to be the first into the market for that particular season, and European ships of all nations continued to use it despite the safety warnings.

At 7.30 a.m. the wind was blowing hard from the north-west and there was a heavy swell on the sea. On board the *Indiana* the east point of Gaspar Island (Pulau Gelasa) was observed bearing north-west by north at a distance of about 2.4km. Gaspar Island was a tiny outcrop of barren rock measuring no more than three kilometres across but rising steeply to over 200 metres above sea level, and visited only by the occasional fisherman. For a brief moment the look-out on the *Indiana* could hardly believe his eyes. Gaspar Island appeared to be surrounded by numerous small rocks protruding above the water, representing a new and unexpected threat to the ship's safety. These rocks had not been mentioned by Lieutenant Ross during his exhaustive survey of the area. The look-out wondered whether he was suffering from tropical delusions. Sometimes fish spawn could look like shoals which suddenly appeared and then disappeared just as speedily. But this was not fish spawn. He informed Captain Pearl of what he had observed. Sails were reefed, and the ship bore up in order to establish more clearly the exact nature of the danger. The rocks appeared to be moving towards them. Then it became evident that they were not rocks at all but numerous pieces of driftwood of every conceivable variety. Boxes, lengths of bamboo, bundles of umbrellas, all kind and manner of debris came gradually into view, a huge floating mass of flotsam and jetsam, bobbing close together on the surface of the sea. And clinging to all this wreckage, struggling in the water, were enormous numbers of people. Each bundle of umbrellas or length of cane supported one or two wretched humans, clearly of Chinese origin. The larger planks of wood had four or six Chinese attached to them. In Captain Pearl's own words, 'I discovered the sea covered with humans for many miles'.

It was immediately evident to all on board the *Indiana* that some appalling catastrophe must have taken place in the immediate vicinity of Gaspar Island. Captain Pearl, without a second thought for his own safety or commercial interests, hove the ship to and ordered the ship's boats to be lowered and manned with his best officers and seamen in order to try and save those who were struggling in the water. 'It was not for me to enquire who they were. They were in distress and must perish but for my aid.' At the same time, he took the precaution of instructing his men not to be diverted from their humanitarian efforts by the lure of easy pickings. Floating wreckage was always a temptation to a poor seaman. Shipwrecked goods were traditionally regarded as part of the providence of God, and little thought was usually given to original ownership. However, in the immediate circumstances of hundreds

Photograph of Gaspar Island. (Dave Moran, 1999.)

of drowning people, Captain Pearl was adamant that all energies were to be directed to the saving of life, not property.

It was hard and dangerous work, pulling the unfortunate Chinese from the sea, ferrying them back to the side of the *Indiana*, and then hoisting them aboard. The weather was deteriorating, with the waves mounting steadily higher and threatening at any moment to capsize the small lifeboats. There was also always the danger that those who were drowning, in their desperation to clamber to safety into one of the rescue boats, might overturn that same boat and all its occupants. The rescue was indisputably a bold and dangerous undertaking.

At 9.15 the weather suddenly deteriorated with a violent squall of wind and heavy rain. The *Indiana* began to drift rapidly to the leeward of Gaspar Island, that is in a southerly direction, and out of contact with the main area of shipwrecked people. Captain Pearl responded immediately by ordering all the remaining sails on the *Indiana* to be taken in, and immediately anchored the ship with the small-bower anchor in 25 fathoms (45.7m) of water to stop it drifting still further away from the drowning Chinese. The problem was that an unanchored ship would drive much faster before the wind, even with the sails taken down, than would a man clinging to a bundle of sticks. The two lifeboats, propelled as they were by oars, were possessed of greater manoeuvrability and were better able to stay on station. They continued to rescue the people in the sea but now, as an added safety measure, the boats were themselves attached to ropes which were veered out from the anchored ship some 200 fathoms or 365metres. The purpose of these ropes was to prevent the boats from also being driven to leeward. If this had happened, and the sailors became too exhausted to row back to the ship in the heavy seas, there was the distinct possibility that the boats might lose contact with the *Indiana* for ever.

As some of the people in the water floated past, the men who were still on board

The South China Sea is a vast area of relatively shallow water, threaded with reefs, which have made it extremely hazardous for shipping for thousands of years. (Wreck Reef, William Westall, 1850, National Maritime Museum, London.)

ship threw ropes for those in the water to try and catch hold of. But this was a last, desperate measure and the chances of success were slim. Captain Pearl in his log-book sombrely recorded the following:

Every person on board the ship employed, heaving ropes to the men on the floats as they approached the ship; many of the latter, from the violence of the wind and sea, were forced from their hold on the floats, and sank to rise no more in our sight, without a possibility of our being able to assist them; others, after getting hold of ropes, were in so exhausted a state that they shared the same fate, and many passed the ship and boats without our having power to assist them.

At eleven o'clock the weather calmed down, and Captain Pearl was able to untether the boats and send them to pick up those people that could still be seen in the water on either side of the ship. At noon the boats returned with 12 more rescued people. The number of those rescued was now counted and came to 95. Communication was difficult owing to mutual incomprehension of each other's languages, but as far as Captain Pearl could gather the shipwrecked people came from a junk that had apparently been wrecked on the north side of Gaspar Island. The rescued Chinese were mostly naked, and so were supplied with spare clothing from the slop clothing that was carried on the ship. They were also provided with 'every kind of refreshment it was proper for them to have in their weak and exhausted state', probably a little boiled rice and water.

At 1 p.m., after a short rest and some food, Captain Pearl sent the boats off yet again to row and sail their way around to the north, or weather side, of the island in order to try and save any more of the junk's people that may have washed up on that side. It took some hours for the boats to get there against the wind and the current, but eventually, in a deep bay on the north-western part of Gaspar, they could see on the rocks of the shoreline a large number of Chinese huddled together and gesticulating frantically. The problem was that the sea was far too rough on this side of the island for the boats to approach the shore with any degree of safety. By means of elaborate signs they indicated to the Chinese that they should move themselves to the south side of the island, which was more protected and would allow an approach to be made. This the castaways did and the boats went in and took off 45 more people, many of them badly cut and bruised from when they had first washed up. There were many more than 45 survivors on the island, and there was the obvious danger that the boats might have been rushed in a sudden panic when those who were being left behind realised what was happening. However, fortunately, one of the newly rescued, called Baba Chy, spoke some Malay and, as some of the crew of the *Indiana* also spoke Malay, a certain level of communication was achieved. It was explained to those Chinese who were being left behind that they were not being abandoned but would all be taken off in due course. And as a proof of the good faith of the rescuers, all the water in the boats was left with those on the island. Gaspar Island itself had no obvious source of fresh drinking-water, though fresh water is indicated in a chart of 1890. The boats returned to the *Indiana* by sundown, by which time the weather was again deteriorating, with hard wind and rain still blowing from the north-west. The achievements of the day are perhaps best summed up in Captain Pearl's own simple words: 'hoisted in the boats for the night and administered all the comfort in our power to the people saved, amounting at this time to 140'.

Baba Chy was now interviewed, with the help of the Malay interpreters. He was the son of a wealthy Chinese merchant living in Batavia, who had been sent back to China for his education and had been returning on board the *Tek Sing* to Batavia to rejoin his parents. It was established from Baba Chy's account that the wrecked junk was of a very large size, 'carrying 1600 passengers aged between 6 and 70', besides a large crew and a valuable cargo. The junk had left Amoy on 14 January and had struck on some rocks situated about nineteen kilometres NNW of Gaspar Island on the evening of the 5th of February. Captain Pearl rightly identified these rocks as being the Belvidere Shoals (Kar Belvidere). According to Baba Chy, the captain of the junk had not been aware of the existence of these rocks. They had been laid down in European charts at least since 1817, but the Chinese, however, were renowned for navigating by means of observation, experience and the compass,

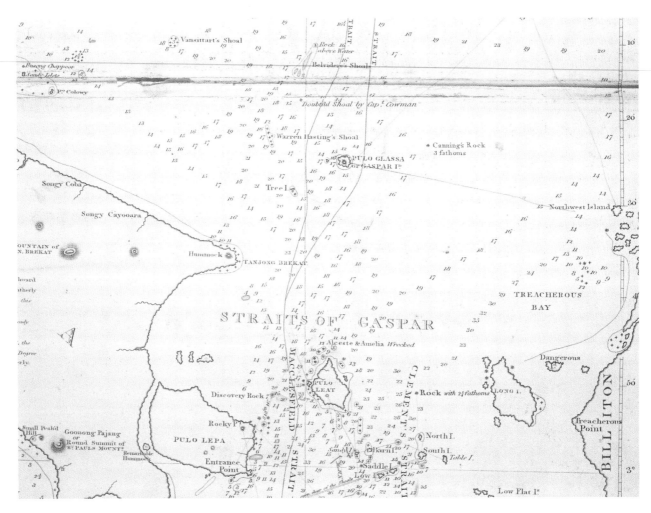

This chart, by James Horsburgh, dated 1819 and published by Norie, is one of the first to show the Belvidere Reef clearly marked. (University Library, Cambridge.)

without reference to charts at all. As this was not a familiar track for Chinese junks it seems quite probable that neither Captain Io Tauko, nor his pilots, had been aware of the existence of the Belvidere Shoals. Also, approaching them after dark, as he was, it is unlikely that the look-out man would have seen shoal water.

Whatever the explanation, the junk had clearly struck the reef with great force, which suggests that it had been travelling at a good speed before a strong northerly wind, probably sailing at something approaching seven or eight knots. Immediately it struck, the junk had heeled right over onto its side, throwing the greatest part of the people on board into the water before they hardly knew what had happened to them. Once in the sea, they grabbed at whatever immediately came to hand. A lot of the light cargo such as bundles of umbrellas and canes that had been lashed to the deck also went straight into the sea. It was these items that some of the drowning Chinese managed to get hold of and cling to for the next 36 hours, drifting during that time some 24 kilometres, before the lucky few were rescued by the efforts of Captain Pearl and his crew. The junk, meanwhile, after beating against the rocks for about an hour, came off and floated into what is described as 'very deep water'. We now know that the depth of water it came into was about thirty metres, which was very deep in those days, certainly beyond salvageable depths. As it beat over the reef the junk came upright again, but almost immediately sank because of the severity of the damage to the hull. It ended up just over a kilometre from the Belvidere Shoals. As it sank, those who still remained on deck also floundered desperately for anything they could cling to.

On board the *Indiana*, on the morning of Friday, 8 February, they made an early start. The wind was much abated, and at 4 a.m. the two boats, commanded by the ship's officers, set off again for Gaspar Island, to rescue the remainder of the people that they had left behind the previous evening. Before accomplishing this, however, just as it grew light they spotted a raft drifting towards them, constructed from two large yard-arms from the junk, with 27 men clinging desperately to it. Originally this raft had had 47 men on it, but it had turned over during the night and twenty men had at that point lost their grip and been too weak to regain it. It seems that these men had spent the first 24 hours after the shipwreck clinging to the masts of the junk, before abandoning it on their makeshift raft. They were now taken off the raft and into the safety of the boats. The boats then fetched off the remaining ten men that had been left on the island at the south-west point the evening before, and returned to the *Indiana*.

At eleven o'clock that same morning Captain Pearl set off himself in the boats, together with his most experienced seamen, this time to go back to the north side of the island. There he observed that there were a number of Chinese still clinging to rocks who were unable to get themselves to the lee side of the island. With great skill and seamanship and at considerable risk to those involved, the boats approached the rocks, despite the size and force of the waves breaking against them, and managed to get in close enough to rescue those who were still trapped. Captain Pearl then rowed round the entire island, landing at several different places, fetching off thirteen more people, all of them badly cut and bruised, until he was satisfied that there was no one else left alive on the island. It was a grisly scene that greeted him. Everywhere he landed there were people lying dead, some of them having drowned before they washed up, others having been beaten to death against the rocks, all of the corpses badly mutilated.

Finally, together with Mr King, one of the ship's officers, Captain Pearl climbed to a height of about 150 metres on the northern side of the island, and scanned the horizon with his telescope, or 'spying glass' as he called it. He could see nothing. There was no trace of any wreckage. If it weren't for

When James Pearl climbed to the top of the hill on Gaspar Island he would have used a spying glass much like this one, made by W.C. Cox of Devonport, c. 1840. National Maritime Museum, London.)

the evidence of the bodies on the shorelines it was as if nothing had happened. Looking towards Belvidere Reef there was now just a smooth and empty sea.

Captain Pearl returned at sundown to the *Indiana*, with the boats and the remainder of those who had been rescued. He now set about counting the number of new mouths he had to feed. The total number of shipwrecked persons was 190. In Captain Pearl's own words, he 'supplied them all with clothes, and every other necessary their distressed situation required'. The entire lower deck of the *Indiana* was cleared in order to accommodate those who had been rescued, and a special area was set aside for those who had been badly gashed and wounded on the rocks of Gaspar Island. Captain Pearl himself, together with another officer, cleaned and dressed everyone's wounds twice a day for the next week and a half.

The *Indiana* now resumed its voyage, heading for Pontiana on the west coast of Borneo. Captain Pearl's decision to continue towards Borneo was an interesting one. Batavia and Pontiana were almost equidistant with each other from Gaspar Island. However, whereas Batavia was only approximately three days' sailing away, because of the favourable northern monsoon winds, reaching Pontiana would take the best part of one week, and if the weather was particularly bad it could take much longer than that. In view of the limited supplies of water and food on board – there were only nine casks of water remaining – this decision was something of a risk. But it is not difficult to understand Captain Pearl's motivation. He was no doubt very aware that he still had a valuable cargo of opium on board that he desperately needed to sell in Borneo. He had already lost two valuable trading days. He could not possibly backtrack all the way to Batavia and then set out for Borneo. That would put at least an extra fortnight on his voyage, possibly much longer.

As the *Indiana* tacked slowly but steadily in a north-easterly direction towards one of the least explored, and most pirate-infested, parts of the world, further details of the shipwreck gradually emerged. One of those that had been saved from the makeshift raft was the second captain of the *Tek Sing*. He confirmed that when the raft left the junk there were no other persons still alive on the wreck. He also provided interesting details of a second, smaller junk called the *Capella Mera*, also known as the 'Red Head', that had been sailing in company with the *Tek Sing* when the latter struck on the reef. He was very bitter about this second junk because it had not stopped to help any of the shipwrecked from the *Tek Sing* but had just continued on its way.

The name 'Capella Mera' sounds Portuguese or Dutch rather than Chinese but has no obvious meaning. The nickname 'Red Head', on the other hand, is rather more revealing. Redhead was the name given to junks whose prows were painted red. Junks from Canton all had red prows by regulation. This would strongly suggest that the second junk that was being referred to by the survivors was the wangkang of Tjieuw Kingliang.

An Ilanun pirate. When a ship was wrecked in the area of the Gaspar Straits, pirates, such as the one depicted here, would descend on it, pillage what cargo was accessible, and, if the hull was stuck on the reef, they would set fire to it in order to extract the ironwork. The Tek Sing *sank too quickly and in too deep water to be plundered by pirates. (From Frank Marryat,* Borneo and the Indian Archipelago, *1848, University Library, Cambridge.)*

*Chinese junk, under sail, with stormy sky in background. (Chinese
School, 19th century, National Maritime Museum, London.)*

Above: Penetrating into the interior of Borneo, to the Chinese gold-mining town of Montradok, involved a journey through swamp and jungle, along a path of felled trees. (From Carl Bock, The Headhunters of Borneo, *1881, University Library, Cambridge.)*

Right: Native in canoe, with bamboo outrigger, threatened by a wounded shark. (William Alexander, 1793, India Office Library.)

Fortunately for all those on board the *Indiana*, the weather for the remainder of the voyage was relatively favourable. On 15 February, that is six days after leaving Gaspar Island, Captain Pearl anchored at the mouth of the Pontiana River. Even then it was to be another four days before the Chinese could be finally disembarked. The town of Pontiana was some nineteen kilometres up the river and could only be approached by ship's boat. There was a large sandbank at the river's mouth which had to be carefully negotiated. Beyond the sandbank the river was over 1.5km wide and fast flowing. Dense vegetation came right down to the river's edge on both sides. The trees, some of which grew to a great height, were swarming with monkeys. The occasional native prahu was the only craft to be seen. To call Pontiana a town was something of an exaggeration. The Dutch Residency was really nothing more than a poor collection of low wooden buildings covered in a crude grass thatch. The Chinese campong formed the only street in the place and that was just a dirt track. The huts of the native Malays were either raised on wooden posts at the edge of the river or were situated on floating pontoons. The Dayaks were not to be seen at all. They were notoriously reclusive and secretive and mainly inhabited the inland forests and waterways, rarely visiting the coastal areas. There was a total absence of roads. All communication was by means of sea or river.

Captain Pearl had not originally intended to visit Pontiana. The real business to be done was further up the coast away from the watchful eye of the Dutch Commissioner. As a commentator in a Bengal newspaper put it at the time, 'Sinkawan is a place of far more importance than either Pontianak or Sambas [the two Dutch outposts], being the principal mart for gold and the best market for the sale of opium and Bengal piece goods on the coast'. Sinkawan, called San Cowan by the Europeans, was controlled by the Chinese. The only reason for calling at Pontiana was to hand over the shipwrecked Chinese to the Dutch authorities. Captain Pearl's reasoning was straightforward. The Chinese emigrants were fleeing from their homeland and wishing to put themselves under the protection of the Dutch Government in Java where they had friends and family. They did not wish to be abandoned on the shores of Borneo where they would

Overleaf: A town in Borneo. (From Frank Marryat, Borneo and the Indian Archipelago, *1848, University Library, Cambridge.)*

Below: A Dayak boy. (From Carl Bock, The Headhunters of Borneo, *1881, University Library, Cambridge.)*

Entrance to a Borneo river, with dense vegetation on both banks. (Admiral Sir Edward Inglefield, National Maritime Museum, London.)

most probably end up working as bonded labourers in the gold-mines. However, Captain Pearl did not want the expense nor the trouble of taking them all to Batavia. Bringing them to Pontiana had already left him significantly out of pocket to the tune of £10–15. The obvious solution was to hand the Chinese over to the representative of the Dutch Government on Borneo, no doubt telling the unfortunate emigrants that the Dutch Commissioner would see that they were safely transferred to Java. That way he would be discharging a duty and also avoiding a future problem. Let the Dutch decide what to do with them.

Captain Pearl was no doubt aware that by calling at Pontiana he was alerting the Dutch to the presence of a foreign trader in waters that the Dutch regarded as their own. He was therefore exposing himself to possible demands for import taxes on the goods he carried. He no doubt kept very quiet about the 175 chests of opium that he had in his holds. He knew that the Borneo coastline was a long one and the Dutch had very few men and ships with which to patrol it. And if there were to be any problems then the Dutch Resident in Borneo had in the past usually been amenable to a small bribe. What he had clearly not reckoned on were the latest dramatic developments in the struggle for power between the Dutch and the Chinese at Sinkawan, nor on the unyielding character of J.H. Tobias, the new Dutch Commissioner in Pontiana.

The Dutch had become increasingly concerned of late that Borneo represented a leaky hole in the trading monopoly that they were still desperately trying to maintain over the entire region. More and more Chinese junks were stopping at Sinkawan and fewer and fewer were coming to Batavia. And to make matters worse, European ships were now also trading into Borneo waters in ever-increasing numbers, particularly the English. Clearly, from the Dutch perspective, this situation could not be allowed to continue. J.H. Tobias, His Netherlands' Majesty's Commissioner for the Island of Borneo, had been dispatched to put an end to what the Dutch perceived as contraband trade. It is not clear whether Commissioner Tobias directly confronted Captain Pearl as to whether he had other business in Borneo waters apart from the landing of the shipwrecked Chinese. But he must have been suspicious. By coming into Pontiana Captain Pearl had inadvertently drawn the attention of the newly vigilant Dutch authorities to his business.

Meanwhile, boats were sent to the *Indiana*, still anchored at the river mouth, and on 19 February the shipwrecked Chinese were finally disembarked. As they left his care Captain Pearl showed some justified pride in their improved condition: 'I am now happy to state that all of them were in good health, and that there were only four

Junk with awning over stern. (J.H. Drummond, early 19th century, National Maritime Museum, London.)

whose wounds had not healed.' But it must have been very confusing for the Chinese, still traumatised by the horrors of the shipwreck. They had originally expected to meet friends and family in Batavia and commence a new life working in Java's sugar and coffee plantations. Now they were being unloaded on an island far more primitive than Java, and would most probably end up working in the gold-mines.

Captain Pearl and Commissioner Tobias had a courteous exchange of letters dated 22 and 23 February. Tobias was fulsome in his praise of Pearl's behaviour: 'I will not hurt your feelings, sir, by thanking you for what you have done. I can only congratulate you that Providence has been pleased to put you in the way of saving so many of your fellow creatures, who, without your generous endeavours would almost certainly exist no more.' The language used by both men is highly revealing. Firstly it is acknowledged by both of them that the Chinese had left their country of birth to 'put themselves under the protection of the Dutch government'. This supports the idea that the Chinese were regarded not just as migrant workers but as economic and political refugees. On a more personal level it is also clear from Tobias's reply that Captain Pearl was becoming concerned about just who was going to compensate him for his humanitarian efforts. Clearly it was of no use looking to the Chinese themselves because they had already lost everything. It is evident that Pearl must have asked Tobias for some financial recompense. Tobias had clearly refused. His remarks

A Tanka boatwoman. The Tanka people were one of the poorest groups of Chinese and it is people of this class who probably formed the majority of the Tek Sing's *passengers. (George Chinnery, 1846, Martyn Gregory Gallery, London.)*

quoted above can be seen as an oblique way of saying that Captain Pearl should look for his reward in heaven and not on this earth. Tobias did, however, agree to put Pearl's case before 'His Excellency the Governor General'. In other words, Tobias adopted the standard excuse of the bureaucrat: he could do nothing himself but he would refer Captain Pearl's case higher up. Pearl had no choice but to accept this decision. He was no doubt still hoping that his personal bravery and humanitarian behaviour would be appropriately recompensed once the story of his efforts became better known. Besides which, the extent of his losses at this stage was relatively modest. He was probably no more than £50 out of pocket and was still anticipating a handsome profit on the sale of his opium. When he wrote to Tobias he can have had little idea of the extent of the financial disaster that lay ahead of him, though it is possible that disturbing rumours were already beginning to circulate.

Ten of the shipwrecked chose not to leave the *Indiana* but expressed a wish to be taken to Batavia. Captain Pearl apparently acceded to their wishes. Again Pearl does not spell it out in his report but there can be little doubt that these ten would have been members of the merchant class or he would surely have insisted on their being off-loaded in Borneo together with the rest of the emigrant workers. It is probable that these ten favoured Chinese promised to pay him for their passage and possible that they even promised to compensate him to some extent when they had made contact with their family members. Whatever promises were made, they were clearly

This painting of an opium clipper illustrates the huge press of sail these vessels carried for their tonnage, which enabled them to sail at speed. The rig of the Indiana *was probably very similar to what is displayed here. (Anon., 19th century, Martyn Gregory Gallery, London.)*

not fulfilled, or if they were they fell far short of Captain Pearl's expectations. Indeed, it is not at all clear that Pearl ever took them to Batavia because the port he next turned up at, later in 1822, was Singapore.

The letters of Tobias and Pearl are interesting as much for what they don't say as for what they do. Shortly before Captain Pearl arrived at Pontiana the Dutch Government had decided to impose a duty of £100 on every chest of opium sold in Borneo. This was extortionate, even by the current standards of taxes on opium, and was clearly designed to put an end to the trade in any ships other than Dutch ones. The Chinese community at Sinkawan, which numbered approximately 60,000 people if those who worked the mines in the hinterland at Montradok were

Portrait of a sea-captain studying a chart. Chinese pilots did not generally use charts; instead they kept close to the coast, following familiar landmarks. (The Chinese artist Lamqua, early 19th century, Martyn Gregory Gallery, London.)

included, was very unhappy about the latest Dutch moves and was quickly up in arms in protest. The Dutch had responded by blockading Sinkawan with their gunboats to all 'foreign' shipping – Chinese junks, Malayan prahus, and English 'country' ships alike. This was the political maelstrom that Captain Pearl blundered into when he pulled up the river at Pontiana in late February 1822, but it was only when he reached Sinkawan that he discovered for himself the full hopelessness of his situation.

Recriminations

WHILE THE *INDIANA* was heading up the South China Sea towards Borneo, in Batavia the Chinese community was anxiously awaiting the arrival of this season's junks bringing relatives and friends, news from the homeland, and a variety of much-desired commodities ranging from sewing needles to cooking woks. The first junks usually appeared on the horizon around the beginning of February, having departed from China one month beforehand. The seaward view from Batavia was stunningly beautiful. The sea was festooned with tiny islands covered with verdant foliage. They were called the Thousand Islands because they were too numerous to count. Between them, scudding at great speed, were hundreds of native fishing prahus with bright yellow sails. These prahus could travel so fast before the wind that the native Javanese who sailed them found it necessary to employ large wooden planks as outriggers, on which some of the crew balanced precariously, to stop the boat from capsizing. The immediate view from the sea, however, was somewhat deceptively charming. The town itself, once a graceful mosaic of elegant houses and canals, that had been described as the 'Queen of the East', had been notorious for years past as a pestilential hole. Its swampy surrounds bred noxious vapours that caused an extremely high mortality among Europeans and natives alike. So dire was the death-rate that anyone

Left: Malay prahus with outriggers. (Thomas & William Daniell, 1810, India Office Library.)

83

Batavia castle and wharf. The castle was originally built in the early seventeenth century. (School of Johannes Rach, 1815, India Office Library.)

Batavia church. (Samuel Drummond, early 19th century, India Office Library.)

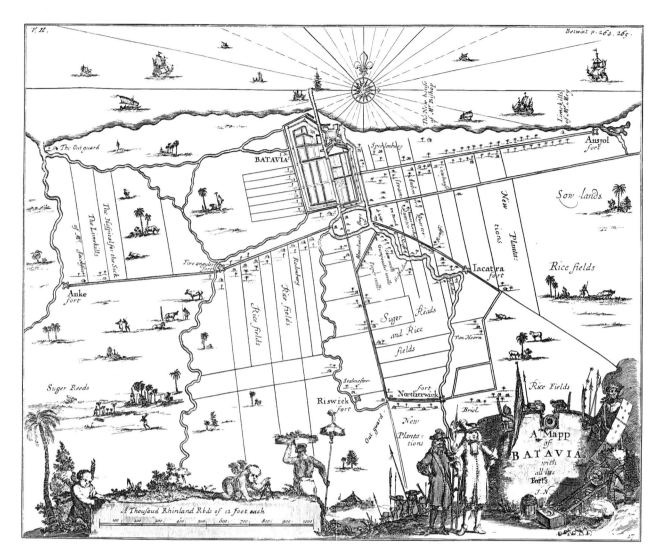

who could afford it had moved to the higher surrounding land, abandoning old Batavia to its ghosts and the poor.

On 10 February 1822 a Chinese wangkang from Canton appeared in the offing of Batavia Anchorage. As soon as its identity had been confirmed, the information spread like wildfire through the Chinese campong, and before many minutes had elapsed every conceivable form of small boat was setting sail in the direction of the junk. Fruit sellers, message carriers, transport boats for the wealthier passengers, they all clustered around the junk's sides, eager to do business. Much shouting took place between the high decks of the junk and the small boats far below, as merchants and traders, family and friends attempted to communicate with each other. Eventually the wangkang came to anchor in the inner harbour and the more important passengers disembarked first into the waiting sampans or prahus. The wangkang had 198 passengers on board. A few were wealthy merchants, but the majority were

Map of Batavia showing the Chinese quarter to the south-east of the castle. (J. Nieuhoff, 1665.)

Overleaf: Approach to Batavia from the sea. (Samuel Drummond, early 19th century, India Office Library.)

penniless emigrants arriving in a strange land with just a mat, a pillow and a bundle of clothes as their sole possessions. The small boats laden with the new immigrants entered the river mouth between two large stone piers that extended into the sea for about 1.5km in an attempt to increase the river's current and reduce the build-up of detritus. On the banks of the river, languid alligators snapped at the waste from the slaughterhouses further upstream. Gangs of chained convicts were used as forced labour to dredge the mud from the river bottom. It was a somewhat inauspicious scene with which to start a new life.

After the passengers had been disembarked, the merchants erected a makeshift roof across the vacated deck space and the contents of the junk's holds were brought up for sale. Before any transactions could take place, however, the entire cargo was assessed by customs officials and the appropriate duties levied. Several hundred years earlier the junk's nachoda would have presented the harbour-master with a bundle of umbrellas and some oranges and this would have been regarded as sufficient dues. Dutch import duties had become rather more burdensome since then.

Interior of a wealthy merchant's house, with porcelain ornaments. (Chinese School, c. 1800, India Office Library.)

Chinese funeral procession in Batavia. (School of Johannes Rach, late 18th century, India Office Library.)

Usually the arrival of a junk was the occasion of great celebration among the Chinese community and would have been accompanied by the beating of gongs and much feasting and dancing. On this occasion, however, the celebrations were somewhat subdued. Even as the wangkang had approached the harbour, a most disturbing rumour had gone round. Another junk called the *Tek Sing* had been wrecked. Many lives had been lost. Sixteen survivors from the *Tek Sing* disaster were on board the wangkang. Gradually more details leaked out. There were not sixteen survivors but eighteen. And they had been picked up clinging to part of a mast near the island of Pulau Leat on the morning of 6 February. The general conclusion was that the *Tek Sing* had been lost on Discovery Rock, which was where HMS *Alceste* was thought to have wrecked some five years previous, returning from Canton with Lord Amherst on board after the latter's disastrous diplomatic mission to China.

According to information brought by the junk's captain, named in the papers as Jalang Lima, the eighteen survivors had been picked up in the vicinity of Pulau Leat some 32 kilometres south of Gaspar Island. It does not seem credible, however, that

The Dutch fleet in Java in 1676, when Dutch power in the region was in its heyday, and before the pollution of Batavia from the sugar-cane plantations. (Anon., National Maritime Museum, London.)

some of those who had been shipwrecked could have drifted as far south as Pulau Leat, 24 hours before Captain Pearl found other survivors drifting in the vicinity of Gaspar Island. There are a number of similar inconsistencies about Jalang Lima's story. But what is most revealing is his statement that he knew nothing of the route through the Gaspar Straits and had simply followed the *Tek Sing*. This surely identifies this wangkang as the 'Red Head' junk that was mentioned by Baba Chy as travelling in tandem with the *Tek Sing*. It also strongly indicates that Jalang Lima and Tjieuw Kingliang were one and the same person. It does not explain why, when they picked up the eighteen survivors, they didn't anchor up and search for the remainder. Were they simply in too much of a hurry to get to Batavia and be the first junk into that season's market, which would have given them a tremendous commercial advantage, particularly as the entire cargo of the *Tek Sing* had been lost? Or were they afraid that the hundreds of emigrants on board the bigger junk would swamp the smaller ship? The exact truth will never be known. But clearly there appears to have been a distinct lack of effort on the part of the captain of the wangkang to rescue as many of the survivors as he might have done.

As soon as news of the disaster reached the ears of the Batavian authorities, a fast-sailing British barque called the *Maryann Sophia*, under the direction of Captain R. Cornfoot, which had recently arrived from Madras, was dispatched to the Gaspar Straits to see whether there were any further Chinese possibly stranded on the

90

islands. The *Maryann Sophia* left Batavia harbour on 13 February with some of those who had been picked up by the wangkang on board, and also the captain of the wangkang. Once in the vicinity of Pulau Leat it became obvious to Captain Cornfoot that the wreck had not taken place where the Chinese captain said it had. But the various accounts provided were so confused that Cornfoot could not be sure where the wreck had happened. All that he could be certain of was that there was no evidence of any other survivors. The *Maryann Sophia* left the Gaspar Straits on 21 February and was back in Batavia by the 23rd with the grim news that of the nearly two thousand people on board it appeared that only eighteen had survived. At that point, of course, nothing was known in Batavia about Captain Pearl and the *Indiana* and the other 190 people who had been rescued.

Meanwhile, Captain Pearl himself was in despair. After leaving Pontiana and sailing up the Borneo coast, he discovered at first hand that the Dutch were indeed blockading all the possible harbours where any free trade with the Chinese might be conducted. In this dire situation he decided to head for Singapore in order to off-load his opium cargo there. Singapore had been founded in 1819 by Sir Stamford Raffles as a free trade port under the control of the British, and in 1821 the first Chinese junk had arrived for the purposes of trade. However, as an entrepôt it was still very much in its infancy and was quite unable to absorb the glut of opium that

Javanese Malays. Despite the sensitivity of their depiction in this painting, native Javanese were generally despised by the colonial Europeans. (Thomas & William Daniell, 1810, India Office Library.)

no doubt came its way as a result of the Borneo impasse. Captain Pearl quickly discovered that he was only able to sell his opium at a severe discount to the original price that he had paid for it. In these circumstances it is understandable, though not entirely logical, that he should have taken the view that his losses were entirely a result of his stopping to help the shipwrecked Chinese. He no doubt felt that if he hadn't stopped, and then deviated to Pontiana, he might have arrived at Sinkawan before the blockade was put into effect. He was later to write that 'this necessary deviation from my voyage in the cause of humanity was the ruin of my speculation'. This might not necessarily have been the case, but it is all too human that he should have seen events in this light.

The effect of this entire episode on Captain Pearl's mental composure was clearly devastating. Not only did he find it difficult to forget the sight of all those Chinese corpses drifting in the sea, he also considered that he was being personally punished for his own humanitarian act. Fourteen years later and residing in Liverpool, he was still trying to claim compensation for his losses from the Chinese and desperately writing to James Matheson, the leading English merchant in Canton, asking him to intervene on his behalf:

The first Chinese junk visited Singapore in 1821. Within a few years it was a flourishing free trade centre. (Chinese artist, c. 1850, Martyn Gregory Gallery, London.)

Left: Sir Stamford Raffles, who spent some years as Governor of Java, after Britain seized it from the Dutch during the Napoleonic Wars. In 1819 he was instrumental in establishing a British colony at Singapore. (George Francis Joseph, 1817, National Portrait Gallery, London.)

*James Matheson, who was,
along with his partner
William Jardine, one of the
most successful of the opium
traders. (Henry Cousins after
James Lonsdale, 1837,
National Portrait Gallery,
London.)*

*I beg, as a particular and generous act of kindness, that you will use your powerful influence
through the Hong merchants, or other channel as you may deem proper, to obtain for me the
pecuniary consideration I so much need, in consequence of my ruinous loss, for humanity to the
suffering Chinese.*

He was claiming £11,000, which was his loss 'on the prime cost of my cargo,
besides all expenses attendant thereon, which I never recovered in commerce'. He
had already successfully lobbied the then Foreign Secretary, Lord Palmerston, to
write a letter to the Chinese emperor putting his case. But there had been no

response. This was hardly surprising as the Chinese state did not accept any responsibility for emigrants, regarding them as criminals who had deliberately put themselves outside the state's protection.

In 1837, Captain Pearl's plight was taken up by the Chinese missionary press of the period and for a while he became something of a *cause célèbre*. In best populist style his behaviour was heralded as a wonderful example of 'Christian philanthropy' as opposed to the 'pagan coldheartedness' of the second Chinese junk. In the wave of publicity that followed, James Matheson, the undisputed king of the opium traders, agreed to open up a subscription for him at his Canton office, and it is possible that various small donations from individual merchants came into this fund. However, the only known tangible compensation that Captain James Pearl ever received was a medal commemorating his bravery from the King of the Netherlands.

The Malacca Straits from Strawberry Hill, near Penang. James Pearl sailed this route returning from Singapore to Calcutta, by which time he was already a broken man. (Captain Robert Smith, c. 1821, India Office Library.)

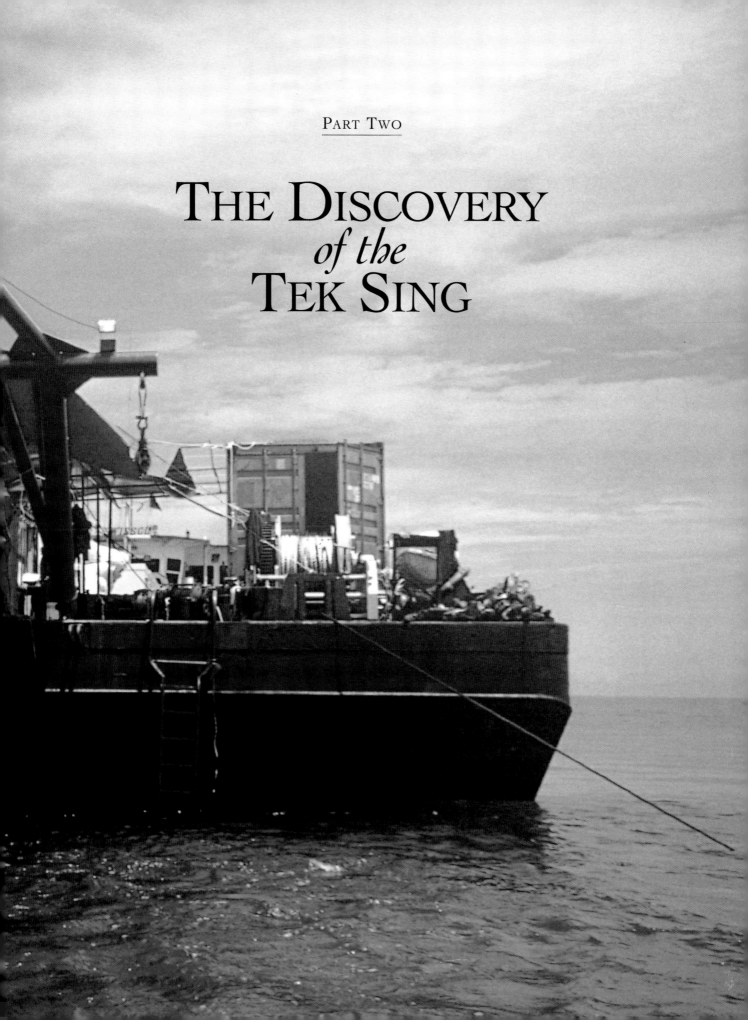

PART TWO

THE DISCOVERY
of the
TEK SING

The Discovery of the Tek Sing

IN APRIL OF 1999 a 25-metre-long motor yacht called the *Restless M* was carefully threading its way in a westerly direction through the tropical paradise that is the Java Sea: tiny uninhabited islands, coral reefs, blue seas and blistering sun. At first glance the *Restless M* looked like most other pleasure launches in this part of the world. Those on board, it might be imagined, were enjoying a luxury cruise, idly fishing for mackerel for their evening meal. But the quantity of antennae bristling from the ship's bridge suggested a different agenda. Indeed, the *Restless M* was equipped with some of the most sophisticated underwater search equipment available in the world, and its quarry was not fish but shipwrecks. It had been investigating in the vicinity of the tiny island of Ternate, one of the first of the Spice Islands to be conquered by the Portuguese, looking for a Portuguese galleon lost in the sixteenth century. The search had been called off in a hurry because the crisis in East Timor had taken a turn for the worse and the safety of the ship and crew was under threat. The image of paradise in this part of the world is something of a chimera.

The search activities of the *Restless M* were financed by an Australian company called Ocean Salvage Corporation, and a number of its crew were also Australian, including the celebrated Michael Hatcher –

Previous pages: The salvage team anxiously await news of the latest finds as the divers resurface. (Dave Moran)

Left: A mound of porcelain lying adjacent to one of the wreck's structural timbers. (Dave Moran)

The Restless M *in quiescent mode. (Ocean Salvage Corporation)*

probably the most successful shipwreck salvor of all time. It was the recovery of the Nanking cargo, blue-and-white porcelain from the Dutch VOC ship *Geldermalsen*, in 1985, that made his name. But before that he had already established a track record in recovering cargoes of tin from World War Two Japanese freighters. However, finding valuable shipwrecks is not an easy business. For every ten thousand wrecks on the ocean floor, only one or two are commercially viable. And since the *Geldermalsen* success, Mike Hatcher had been going through a lean period. The abortive Ternate project was only the last in a series of mishaps and disappointments.

As the *Restless M* and its crew withdrew from the Spice Islands, Mike and I had a series of satellite telephone conversations. We had discussed the reefs to the north of the Gaspar Straits, now called Gelasa Straits, many times before. They were a notorious shipwreck blackspot – I had details of over fifty sinkings on those reefs during the first few decades of the nineteenth century alone. Since Mike already had a search licence for the area from the Indonesian Government, and it seemed that the political troubles in East Timor were far enough away from that particular part of Indonesia not to be a worry, everything pointed to the Gelasa Straits as being our last hope for a successful discovery during the 1999 season.

The Gelasa Straits had first been explored by Europeans towards the end of the eighteenth century. Up until then the vast majority of shipping, both Chinese and European, sailing between China and Java, had gone by the Bangka Straits route. But looking at a chart – even a chart of the eighteenth century – was enough to make it

Mike Hatcher with an earthenware jar. (Dave Moran)

evident that the Gelasa Straits route had the potential for being shorter and faster. And in the increasingly dynamic commercial world of that period speed became more and more of a concern.

The Gelasa Straits route had in fact been known to the Chinese for hundreds of years. It is referred to in a pilot called the *Shun Feng Hsiang Sung* or the *Fair Winds for Escort* written in 1430, the period of the great Zheng He treasure ships, the original manuscript of which can be seen in the Bodleian Library in Oxford. However, despite these early explorations by the Chinese, later on the Gelasa Straits appear to have been abandoned as a useful passage. It was the Bangka Straits route that became the standard for sailing-ships of all nations travelling in both directions. The reasons for the abandonment of the Gelasa Straits route are not clear, but perhaps there were too many casualties during those early years. In the late eighteenth century there was an enormous hydrographic effort, largely undertaken by British captains such as Lestock Wilson in the *Vansittart*, to chart the eastern seas more accurately, and interest in the Gelasa went through a renaissance. However, despite the improved charts, the number of casualties travelling this route remained extraordinarily high at least until the middle of the nineteenth century.

The Belvidere Reef was our particular focus of attention. The reef runs north-east and south-west for a distance of 6.5 kilometres right across the main approach from the north to the Gelasa Straits. At the north-east end a sinister black rock protrudes some two metres above the sea. But for most of its length the reef lurks approximately two metres below the surface, waiting to catch an unsuspecting keel. In calm weather the swell can be seen breaking, but when the weather is rough it is difficult to distinguish the breakers from the white wave spume whipped up by the wind. These problems are compounded when sailing at night, of course. Nor did frequent casting of the lead, in order to establish the depth of water the ship was sailing in, provide an adequate safeguard, because the depths shelve so suddenly there is virtually no warning. Mike and I both knew from Horsburgh's *Sailing Directions* of at least one large ship, a Chinese junk, that had come to grief on the Belvidere, some

A fishing platform off Bangka Island. (Nigel Orloff)

two hundred years previously, and we fully expected to find dozens more. But it was the junk that was of particular interest, with its potential for porcelain and gold.

The *Restless M* was equipped with side-scan sonar, a forward-looking echo sounder and a magnetometer. The sonar and the echo sounder both work on the same principle: a series of sound waves is transmitted towards the sea-bed; whatever these waves hit they then bounce off and the echo or rebound is collected by a responder. This data is then fed into a computer and a picture is produced of the sea-bed terrain showing the hills and the valleys. If a sound wave hits an object such as a wreck then this distorts the sea-bed pattern and the wreck shows up as an anomaly. Obviously, if the wreck is a large iron structure, then the anomaly is a sizeable one and it is not usually difficult to pick it out. However, if the wreck is a wooden one, then it is very probable that it will have been reduced over the years to nothing much more than a hump on the surface of the sea-bed, so making it much more difficult to discern, even using an enhanced computer imaging system. Old wooden shipwreck mounds are not very different in size and shape from rocks and, nine times out of ten, what looks like a shipwreck mound on the screen turns out to be just another lump of granite. If the wooden wreck has been completely covered up by sand, as sometimes happens, then clearly it will not show up on the side-scan at all.

The magnetometer works on a completely different principle, however. All shipwrecks containing ferrous material will have a distorting effect on the magnetic field that surrounds them. The more ferrous material, the bigger the distorting effect. A magnetometer is programmed to record these distortions in the

Local fishing craft moored off Gaspar Island. This is one of the few sandy beaches where it is possible to land and may well have been where Captain Pearl put ashore when attempting the rescue of the Tek Sing *survivors. The dense vegetation has remained unchanged for hundreds of years. (Nigel Orloff)*

Arrasan Sundaram at the search station on the Restless M. *(Dave Moran)*

background magnetic field. Such a device can find wrecks even if they are completely covered by sand, provided they have a sufficient quantity of ferrous metal on them. However, like the side-scan, it frequently mistakes rocks for shipwrecks, although for a different reason: some rocks have magnetic anomalies of their own and, therefore, they distort the magnetometer readings in the same way that a shipwreck would. If the exact quantity of iron on a potential target is known, then it is possible to program the magnetometer readings so that only those within a set spectrum are targeted and rogue readings can be ignored. However, more often than not, the exact quantity of iron is not known and therefore a wide set of parameters has to be employed which will pick up all manner of targets, both geological and man-made. The magnetometer has the further drawback that it cannot cover anywhere near as wide a swathe of sea-bed as does a side-scan sonar. It therefore takes much longer using a magnetometer to check out a given area of sea-bed than it does with a side-scan.

For Mike Hatcher on the *Restless M* the narrowness of the magnetometer swathe was not really a problem because the total search area was relatively small. Even if he searched up to five kilometres from the reef, this would still only give a search area of some 155 square kilometres. And Mike was pretty certain, in his own mind, that the junk would have floated off the reef in a southerly direction. The set of the current combined with the prevailing north-easterly winds suggested to him that this would have been the most likely scenario and, if true, this meant that the search area could be cut in half. It was therefore quite feasible to run the side-scan and the magnetometer at the same time. That way, he maximised his chances of finding something. Unfortunately, it also maximised the chances of finding targets that were of no interest. For weeks the divers went down on images that had shown up on the ship's search instruments, only to find nothing more interesting than modern motor yachts or old fishing trawlers, or even just part of the detritus that litters all the oceans – tin petrol-cans, abandoned anchors, rusting engines. A steel screw steamer from the beginning of the twentieth century, a Macassar schooner, a privately owned American yacht – they were all located, examined and rejected. Old wooden shipwrecks were also found, but none of them contained anything to suggest that it had been a Chinese junk. Few outside the salvage business realise that it is not finding shipwrecks that is the problem: it is finding the *right* shipwreck. And then – something that is often even more difficult – being able to positively identify it *as* the right shipwreck.

Right: The divers worked in teams of two and enjoyed the rare luxury of a lift when descending to the sea-bed. (Dave Moran)

Weeks went past and the *Restless M* continued to chug slowly up and down the seas around the Belvidere Reef, surveying for sixteen hours a day. There came one false hope after another. Those on board had plenty of time to ponder the treacherous nature of the subterranean cliff-face around which they were constantly circling. A careless turn of the wheel and they could all end up as just one more shipwreck statistic. Accurate navigation was also vital because if the lines that the *Restless M* was following wavered just a metre or two, a chink of sea-bed might be missed, and that could be just the place where the target wreck was lying. Fortunately, the *Restless M* was equipped with a DGPS (digital geographic positioning system), which meant that it was always possible to know within a few centimetres exactly where on the planet's surface the ship was at any one time and also where it had been. This was an enormous aid to accurate navigation. Even with the aid of the DGPS, however, surveying was still monotonous work that called for intense concentration. Not for nothing is the process known in salvage parlance as 'mowing the lawn'.

Around the beginning of May, Mike needed to travel to Jakarta in order to sort out some administrative problems with the Indonesians. The searching continued without him. He has a well-trained team of loyal men, led by Abdul Rahim, several of whom have been with Mike for the best part of twenty years. On the evening of 10 May there came up an image on the sonar trace that might just conceivably have been a shipwreck mound. This sparked very little interest on board. There had been too many false alarms during the previous two months for anyone to get excited. Besides, there was only the smallest flicker on the magnetometer. That made it unlikely that it was a shipwreck at all, let alone the right shipwreck. It was already late in the day, too late for making an exploratory dive. And then everyone's attention was distracted when someone shouted that the ship's dinghy had gone missing. This was a serious setback. The next day was spent searching for the missing boat. There was no sign of it. It was possible it had been stolen by passing pirates, but much more likely that it had been carelessly tied up and had just drifted away. It was an embarrassment that the crew would have preferred not to tell Mike about – just one more piece of bad news in what was rapidly turning into a year of nothing but.

It wasn't until the morning of the 12th that Rahim remembered that they still hadn't examined the target they had picked up some 36 hours beforehand. No one was very positive about it, but none the less it still had to be checked out. The *Restless M* anchored up. Before dropping anchor, however, the ship moved a short distance away from the latest target area, in order to avoid dropping several tons of steel into the middle of what might just conceivably have been a cargo of fragile porcelain. After the missing dinghy they couldn't afford any more mishaps. Rahim then donned scuba gear and entered the water with Yono, his diving partner.

The sea floor was about thirty metres down. Although the water was clear, only limited daylight penetrated that far down, so the divers moved in a twilight zone. The

Abdul Rahim's birthday celebrations in the mess room on the salvage barge. (Ocean Salvage Corporation)

One of the large iron mast rings which led to the discovery of the wreck. (Dave Moran)

Below: Stacks of porcelain on the sea-bed just as it had originally been loaded, but without any of the packaging materials which had long since rotted away. (Dave Moran)

first unusual clue they came across was a large iron ring about one metre in diameter. It was followed by another iron ring and then a third – a whole series of iron rings at regularly spaced intervals. It was a curious phenomenon. At first it was not at all clear what their function could have been. Later it was realised that these rings had once been used as metal bands to strengthen a mast of huge proportions. The mast must have been over thirty metres long and more than three metres in circumference, but not a trace of the wood survived. Whatever ship this proved to be, it was clearly of a very large construction. The rings led to a wreck mound some fifty metres long and ten metres wide and, as the divers swam towards it, they caught a glimpse of a piece of blue-and-white porcelain, luminous in the semi-darkness, as pristine as on the day it had first been removed from the kiln. Nor was this just a random find. There were stacks of the stuff rising in a pile more than two metres above the sea-bed. It was an awe-inspiring sight. Could this be the 'big Chinese Junk' mentioned by Horsburgh that they had come to find?

Once Mike heard about the discovery, he wasted no time in getting on a small Fokker F 28 to Bangka airport at Pangkal Pinang and heading straight back to the site. He needed to verify for himself what he had been told on the telephone. It wasn't that he didn't trust his divers, but he had been in the shipwreck business long enough to know how easily people let their imaginations carry them away once beneath the surface of the sea. On this occasion he was not disappointed. The wreck was far bigger than any wooden wreck he had ever set eyes on before. And the quantity of porcelain that confronted him was simply colossal. It made the *Geldermalsen* remains look quite tiny in comparison.

The salvage barge over the wreck site, with Gaspar Island looming in the background. This is the view that the Tek Sing *survivors would have had as they clung desperately to the masts and any available floating objects. (Nigel Orloff)*

Mike stopped only a couple of days at the wreck, selecting a few sample pieces of porcelain for identification purposes, before setting sail again in the *Restless M* for Singapore. Once in Singapore, the porcelain was photographed, and Mike flew to London to talk to Colin Sheaf of Christie's. He also contacted me and asked me whether a Chinese junk could possibly have had a series of iron rings around its mast or whether it was perhaps a European or American ship that he had found.

My own research into the question of the iron rings was quickly answered. In the National Maritime Museum I consulted Audemard's six-volume work on Chinese junks, in the serene surroundings of the Caird Library. Audemard was quite explicit on the subject: Chinese masts were often 'fished together and strengthened by a series of iron collars'. It looked like we had indeed found our junk.

Colin Sheaf's opinion on the porcelain was more puzzling. He thought from the designs on the plates that it was porcelain aimed primarily at the Asian market, which was consistent with it being on a Chinese junk. However, Colin dated the sample we showed him to the middle of the eighteenth century. This didn't fit at all with what I had so far managed to find out about the big Chinese junk lost on the Belvidere. The edition of Horsburgh in which I had first come across a reference to the big junk was the fifth edition of 1843. Early editions of Horsburgh are rare and it was only with difficulty that I was able to track them down – not even the India Office Library has a complete set. The first edition of 1809 made no mention of the big junk, nor did the second of 1817; but the third edition of 1827 did refer to it. This was a strong indication, if not absolute proof, that the junk was lost sometime between 1817 and 1827, a good fifty years after the date to which Colin attributed the porcelain. This seemed to indicate one of two things. Either Colin was wrong about his dating or we had found a different Chinese junk lost some fifty years or more before the Horsburgh junk.

As it turned out, neither of these was the case and there was a third explanation for the inconsistency of dates. Colin had been right: the junk was carrying porcelain, some of which was nearly one hundred years old when it sailed, and it was this older porcelain that Mike had come across first. Indeed, there was porcelain from all periods on the junk, from the fifteenth century through to the nineteenth – all of which indicates just what a difficult process dating shipwrecks can be.

Mike now set about the salvage stage with his customary energy and enthusiasm. The barge *Swissco Marie II* was chartered from Singapore, together with its stablemate tug the *Swissco 88*. The barge is an enormous floating industrial unit sixty metres long and fifteen metres wide, equipped with a fifty-tonne crane, an A frame, decompression chambers, compressors, gas cylinders, and all the paraphernalia of a major dive project. At the rear of the barge is a three-storey accommodation block for up to fifty crew and divers to sleep and relax in, complete with a medical unit, a laboratory and a control centre.

The task that lay ahead was a huge logistical exercise. It involved raising over 300,000 pieces of porcelain from the sea-bed by hand and then documenting, photographing, wrapping and packing into containers each separate piece. The divers worked in teams of two, using Kirby Morgan fibreglass dive helmets and

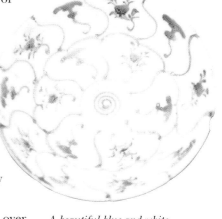

A beautiful blue-and-white saucer dish with a popular central spiral pattern. (Ocean Salvage Corporation)

Each piece of porcelain was individually photographed and documented as it came on board – a colossal logistical exercise. (Dave Moran)

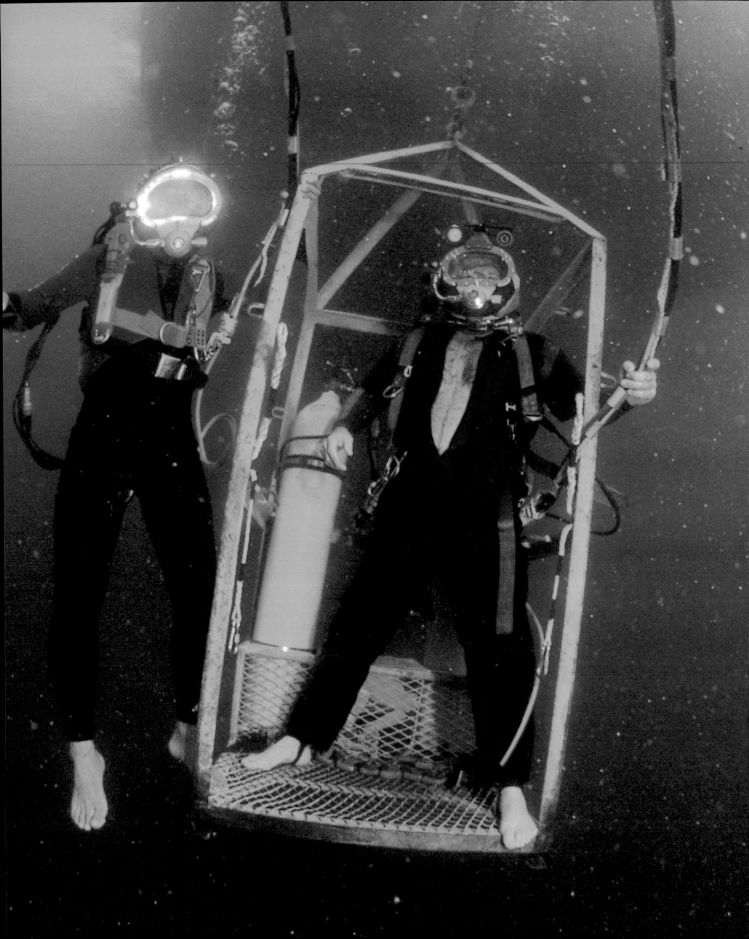

breathing surface-supplied air, which allowed them ninety minutes on the bottom followed by forty minutes in the decompression chamber. The purpose of the decompression process is to allow the nitrogen gases, which would have dissolved into the diver's bloodstream while he was under water as a result of the increased pressure, to become gaseous again in a controlled and harmless manner. Without undergoing this decompression process the diver exposes himself to the risk of the nitrogen gases bubbling out in a rush as he surfaces; this is what causes the notorious and intensely painful condition known as the 'bends', which in extreme cases can be fatal. In total 2,250 man-hours of diving were completed during the salvage phase without any serious accidents, which is a significant tribute to the efficiency of the operation.

As Mike's work of excavation commenced on one side of the world, I continued my own researches in the archives, trying to discover more of the story behind the big junk mentioned by Horsburgh. What had been its name, where had it come from, where was it sailing to, and – particularly intriguing – who was the mysterious 'Captain of a country ship belonging to Calcutta' who had saved 'part of the people' on board? Horsburgh provided no answers to these questions. As explained above, I had narrowed the date of sinking down to some point between 1817 and 1827, and as the captain of the country ship had operated out of Calcutta, I set about reading the *Calcutta Journal* for those years. It was just possible that this valiant captain had made a report of what had happened, which had subsequently been published in the newspapers of the period. So I started on daily trips to the British Library newspaper division at Colindale, London, studying the badly printed microfilms of the pages of the *Calcutta Journal*, hunting for possible clues. It was extremely slow and tedious work and, as some editions of the newspaper were missing, I could not be sure, even if there had been a report, that it had been preserved. From 1817 to 1827 amounts to a colossal quantity of reading matter. I spent several weeks covering the first year alone and it was becoming obvious to me that to complete the whole task would take many months.

It was then that I remembered that while scanning the pages of Audemard, looking for information about the iron rings that Mike had found, I had come across a reference to another large junk being lost. Of course, large junks were being lost all the time and I had dismissed the reference as irrelevant to my purpose because Audemard had stated that this particular junk had been wrecked in Amoy. Our junk had been lost some 3,200 kilometres away. But authors, even ones of serious

Mike Hatcher on an underwater scooter, using subaqua gear. (Dave Moran)

Left: The divers wore Kirby Morgan helmets and breathed air supplied from the surface. (Dave Moran)

academic repute like Audemard, do not always get the details right. Perhaps he had got the place of sinking wrong. Perhaps the junk had not been wrecked *in* Amoy at all but had been coming *from* Amoy. I went back to the National Maritime and looked again at Audemard's remarks on this sinking. He mentioned that the rescue ship, called *Pearl*, had had an English captain and that some of the people on board had been saved. He also mentioned the year of sinking as being 1822. An English captain and the saving of life were both details that were consistent with Horsburgh. The year of sinking was within the Horsburgh parameters. The place of sinking, Amoy, was definitely not consistent, but all the same it seemed worth taking a chance and skipping straight to the year 1822.

Right: A European winebottle recovered from the wreck site. (Ocean Salvage Corporation)

As it turned out, my chancing on the Audemard reference was one of those pieces of luck that the wreck researcher relies on, even though the reference was inaccurate in several important respects. The *Calcutta Journal* for June 1822 carried a full report on the sinking of a big Chinese junk on the Belvidere Reef *en route* from Amoy to Batavia. It was from this report that we first learned of the terrible scale of the disaster and the massive loss of life. The rescue ship's name had not been *Pearl* but *Indiana* – Pearl was, of course, the name of the captain. But Audemard *had* got the year right. From there on, everything began to click into place. The India Office Library yielded a lot more information on Captain Pearl and just what he had been up to on that voyage when he came across the shipwrecked Chinese. And the Dutch archives in The Hague provided more detail on the junk, including the fact that its name had not been *Teck Necun* as reported in the British press, but *Tek Sing* or 'True Star'. It is curious to think that just as the iron rings on the sea-bed floor had led Mike Hatcher to the wreck's final resting-place, so those same iron rings in Audemard had led me to the wreck's true identity.

A heap of porcelain concreted into a single mass. (Dave Moran)

As the excavation of the junk progressed, further questions arose. A number of European winebottles and watches made in London were unearthed. Again this threw some doubt on whether the wreck was after all of Chinese origin. Could it in fact have been a European ship with a Chinese cargo on board? This seemed unlikely. The sheer quantity of Chinese cargo argued against it – not just the porcelain but a host of other artefacts such as cooking woks, hairpins, pigtails, inking pads, all of a specifically Chinese design and manufacture. But then why the European wines and watches? Perhaps there had been European merchants on board when

112

the *Tek Sing* struck so dramatically against the Belvidere Reef. This was an intriguing possibility. Europeans were not allowed in Amoy, but some of the more adventurous of the free-traders had already begun to sail up the coast from Canton looking for new distribution centres for their opium cargoes. Was it possible that some of these merchants found it convenient to return directly to Batavia in a Chinese junk?

A more likely explanation was found in the pages of John Phipps, who published in 1823 an invaluable work called 'A Guide to the Commerce of Bengal'. The scope of the work is much wider than the title implies and it includes extensive lists of articles exported from China during the early years of the 1820s. These items included clarets, port wines and gin, not products that one usually associates with Chinese junks, but clear evidence of the complexities of entrepôt trading at the time. No doubt the Dutch in Batavia got their gin directly from Holland but they must have found it on occasion cheaper to buy their French and Portuguese wines from China rather than through other major trading centres such as Calcutta. It was not for nothing that John Crawfurd, who published an important work on the Indian Archipelago in 1815, described the Chinese who had settled in Java as 'generally engaged in trade, in which they are equally speculative, expert and judicious'.

Another interesting discovery neatly demonstrates the way in which shipwrecks, even if they do not exactly rewrite history, can often qualify and deepen our understanding of the written texts. The *Amoy Gazetteer* of 1834 specifically states that ocean-going ships were only allowed to carry two cannon. No less than seven cannon have so far been discovered at the wreck site. Seven is still a pitifully small number

Above: A watch made in London. Mechanical objects, such as clocks and watches, were a favourite item of export from Britain to China. (Ocean Salvage Corporation)

Left: A bronze Chinese cannon being brought on board the barge. (Ocean Salvage Corporation)

Right: Mike Hatcher lifting a large earthenware jar from the sea-bed. (Dave Moran)

Below: Pots on the sea-bed with amazing displays of coral growth. (Dave Moran)

for an ocean-going ship of this size when compared with the quantity of cannon that a European ship of similar proportions would have carried. But it points up the gap between the Chinese regulation and the common practice. Most of the cannon have been left *in situ* but one particularly beautifully decorated bronze cannon with a flared muzzle has been raised. The presence of the iron cannon had resulted in only a small flicker of the magnetometer because the iron was heavily corroded and the resultant magnetic field had degraded almost to the point of non-existence.

Meanwhile, as the divers continued to carefully excavate the wreck site, penetrating deep below the surface of the surrounding sand and removing tonne after tonne of valuable porcelain, further extraordinary items came to be discovered that continually reminded Mike Hatcher and his team of the terrible tragedy that had taken place all those years before. There was, for instance, a sad irony about part of the ship's ballast. It consisted of granite gravestones. Many of them were blank but some of them already had names engraved on them. These were probably intended for recently deceased relatives in Batavia, but it is also possible that some of the more elderly of the passengers carried their own gravestones with them. The wealthier Chinese were very meticulous about the need for a proper burial in the family tomb and it was obviously important to them that the gravestones used came from their homeland, even if they were to be interred in a foreign country. None of these gravestones was removed from the wreck site. It seemed only appropriate that they should remain as a permanent testimony to all those who had lost their lives.

The subject of gravestones inevitably raises the issue of how does one treat a wreck site which was the scene of such appalling death and destruction. Most of the victims who drowned floated far from the wreck, as is clear from Captain Pearl's testimony. Many of those who died washed up on the shores of Gaspar Island and many more would have ended up on Banca and Pulau Leat. Nevertheless the junk went down at such speed, once it came off from the reef, that there were inevitably those who would have been trapped below deck or crushed beneath fallen timbers. Mike Hatcher made a particular point of insisting that the wreck site was treated with proper respect. The many divers who were involved in the excavation said their own private prayers for those who had perished. The divers were multinational in origin – Indonesians, Malaysians, Australians, New Zealanders, Canadians, French and British. They subscribed to many religions, including Hindu, Moslem and Christian. But divers of all nations are probably more aware of the perils of the sea than most other occupational groups and these instinctively treated the wreck site with an appropriate dignity.

It has been argued by certain people involved with shipwrecks – in particular by Bob Ballard who discovered and filmed the *Titanic* – that shipwrecks are graves and should not be interfered with in any way. Their view is that no artefacts should be recovered (although, interestingly, filming is not regarded as a form of intrusion or interference). However, this inconsistency apart, Mike Hatcher vigorously rejects the 'look and take pictures but don't touch' argument. Firstly, he points out that wrecks are being disturbed all the time not by salvors, but through the activities of massive

Above: An elegant vase. (Ocean Salvage Corporation)

Left: An earthenware dragon teapot – Yixing ware – with an extraordinary encrustation of coral. (Ocean Salvage Corporation)

A large earthenware jar with wonderful coral accretions. (Ocean Salvage Corporation)

Axe heads – the Tek Sing *was full of utilitarian items such as porcelain oil-lamps and earthenware wok ovens. (Dave Moran)*

industries such as the oil and fishing sectors. Pipelines and trawl nets are continually tearing through ancient wreck sites, wreaking untold damage, and the operatives involved are, more often than not, unaware of what is happening. Secondly, the sea-bed itself, even without human interference, is not a stable environment. Natural corrosion combined with the destructive effect of freak storms may destroy overnight a fragile environment that may have preserved a shipwreck for hundreds of years. But perhaps the most important argument in favour of responsible excavation and recovery is that, if legitimate salvage is outlawed, then the activity will go underground and will be run entirely by those operating within the black market. In this scenario unrecorded looting will become the norm and no one will ever know the provenance of the artefacts that will still reach the auction rooms and the antique shops. Responsible salvage increases human understanding and helps to conserve the past. For instance, porcelain experts, who have studied the extraordinary variety of artefacts recovered from the *Tek Sing,* are already claiming that this find is of such significance that it will rewrite the history of Chinese porcelain manufacture. This kind of reappraisal would not be possible without salvaging the porcelain itself.

Apart from gravestones, there were some other large and cumbersome items that were found deep in the ballast. These were stone mill-wheels destined for the sugar-mills of Java. Sugar was one of the first of the major cash crops that the Dutch encouraged the Chinese community in Java to develop. The Chinese had had a presence in Java, brewing arrack and cultivating rice, even before the Dutch first arrived in 1596 under Cornelis de Houtman. But it was only after the Dutch had established Batavia as a military base in 1619 that the Chinese population began to expand rapidly under Dutch protection and encouragement. The sugar plantations

Above: Green and brown porcelain spoons, nearly 2,000 in number, were among the more interesting items recovered. (Ocean Salvage Corporation)

Left: A large millstone, almost certainly destined for use on Java's sugar plantations, and in near-perfect condition. (Ocean Salvage Corporation)

that were subsequently developed were almost entirely run by the Chinese, and many of the poorer emigrants on the *Tek Sing* would have been hoping to find work on them. The Chinese also carried out all the collection of taxes from the indigenous Javanese population, on behalf of the Dutch, using a system known as 'tax farming'. The Dutch found the Chinese to be useful business partners. It was a policy of co-operation and collusion much envied by other European nations. The Englishman, Woodes Rogers, who visited Batavia around the year 1700, observed: 'the Dutch have all Chinese commodities brought to them cheaper than they can fetch them ... it is a

These superb Chinese lion statues would have been used by wealthy merchants to adorn their gateways. (Ocean Salvage Corporation)

pity our East India Company has no settlement to which the Chinese might resort'. It was an astute observation and it was only when Singapore was founded over one hundred years later that this weakness in the British position was fully redressed.

Interestingly, recent research suggests that it was the sugar industry that caused the terrible pollution of the River Ciliwung. The run-off from the milling process poisoned the waters of the river. In the eighteenth century the once-beautiful town of Batavia, with its wide canals and elegant Dutch-style housing, became a virtual death-sentence for those who were posted there. At the beginning of the nineteenth century the old Batavia was largely abandoned and the inhabitants moved to higher ground away from the contaminated river.

The wreck site (like most wreck sites) was rich in natural life. The divers shared their underwater habitat with sting-rays, red snapper, coral trout, squid, barracuda and sharks. But it wasn't the sharks *under* the water that were the main cause of concern. These particular seas were still infested by pirates, just as they had been for centuries past. At night, while the divers slept, there were always two armed guards on the look-out for potential marauders.

Once the bulk of the porcelain had been removed from the *Tek Sing* wreck site, it became possible for Mike Hatcher and his diving team to appreciate more fully the enormous size of the original ship. The wreck mound was over fifty metres long and ten metres wide. There was no wood showing above the sand, but as the excavation progressed a number of giant timbers were revealed that were more than one metre thick. Junks are often thought of as having been built with flat bottoms and, although this is true for those used for river and coastal navigation, it is not true of the ocean-going junks, such as the *Tek Sing*, which had a conventionally rounded lower hull. The *Tek Sing*, however, was very different from the ocean-going Western ship in respect of its keel. In fact, the junk did not have a keel at all, or not at any rate a keel as understood by Western naval architects. What it had instead was a series of hardwood sections fixed to the outside of the hull, known as 'dragon spines'. The main longitudinal strength of the hull was achieved not by the keel but by means of hardwood wales that ran around the ship along the water-line and which created a kind of protruding ledge about one metre wide. The gunwale was also constructed from large timbers and was wide enough to allow the sailors to use it for passage from the fore to the aft of the ship. The large timbers that have been revealed at the wreck site were most probably remnants of the original longitudinal wales, but to date the excavation has not proceeded far enough for this to be confirmed. The seams of the hull would have been caulked with a mixture of burnt and crushed oyster shells, oil from the chinnam tree (known as tung oil) and jute. This forms a putty-like substance which sets hard and is highly waterproof. The hulls of these ocean-going junks were also often double-planked, new planks being nailed over the old ones when the latter were beginning to wear. The hull of the *Tek Sing*, however, was not

Wreck sites are a favourite habitat for fish and the Tek Sing *site is no exception.*
(Dave Moran)

These extraordinary porcelain Chinese boys with their amazingly detailed features are far superior, even to those found on the Geldermalsen *wreck some 70 years earlier, and raise all kinds of questions about the history of Chinese porcelain manufacture. (Ocean Salvage Corporation)*

double-planked, which suggests that it was not that old a junk when it was wrecked. The planks and beams were nailed together with iron and fastened with wooden dowels. A number of iron nails were observed around the wreckage.

In the period that the *Tek Sing* was constructed the majority of Chinese junks were built in Siam (Thailand) where the costs of shipbuilding were significantly lower than in China itself, owing to a plentiful supply of fir and teak. A junk could be built in Bangkok from start to finish in only two months. The Chinese craftsmen did not work from plans but constructed their ships entirely by eye and tradition. The lower hull planking was most usually constructed from fir, with the masts and upper works made of teak and the rudder and anchors from ironwood. Ironwood was a special, highly dense wood obtainable only on Hainan Island and in Borneo. However, sometimes teak, seasoned by keeping it for a long period under marshy water, was used as a substitute for ironwood. The wooden timbers of the junk were left in a far rougher state than their equivalent would have been on a Western ship, the Chinese seeing no point in perfecting something that either was out of sight in the hold or formed part of the outer hull and was therefore likely to be buffeted against rocks and bruised by cannon-shot.

Much of our present-day knowledge concerning the structure of ocean-going junks at the beginning of the nineteenth century comes from the description of a particular junk, called the *Keying*, that was sailed to New York from China, around the Cape of Good Hope, in 1846–7, and then across the Atlantic to London. The captain of this junk was a British entrepreneur called Kellett. It was not permitted for junks to be sold to Westerners and Captain Kellett only acquired the *Keying* through subterfuge and bribery. He was most impressed by its sailing qualities, commenting that throughout numerous storms and gales she 'proved herself an admirable seaboat'. He brought the junk to the West essentially as a publicity stunt, mooring it on the Thames and charging an entrance fee to the curious. The enterprise was highly successful. The junk caused quite a sensation, was featured twice in the *London Illustrated News,* and became part of a vogue for all things Chinese that, somewhat strangely, swept through Britain after the close of the Opium Wars. At the time of the junk's historic voyage it was said to be nearly one hundred years old which, although probably something of an exaggeration, clearly places it very much in the same period as the *Tek Sing*.

According to Kellett, the *Keying*'s main mast measured ninety feet (27.4m) long and was three feet four inches (1m) in diameter at deck level, while the foremast was seventy-five feet (23m) long and one foot six inches (0.45m) in diameter at deck level, and the mizzen mast was fifty feet (15.2m) long. This is largely consistent with the measurements that have been taken at the wreck site, where the main mast of the

A delicate blue-and-white teacup that has survived in perfect condition. (Dave Moran)

Tek Sing appears to have been in excess of 27.4 metres and of a diameter almost identical to the *Keying*'s. This would also tie in with the historical data which refer to the *Tek Sing*'s mast protruding above the surface of the sea some ten feet (3m) at the time of the original sinking, at a water depth of approximately one hundred feet (30m). Allowing for the height of the main deck above the sea-bed, this gives a probable length of the main mast above the deck of 28.7 metres. The *Keying* was a junk of the second class while the *Tek Sing* was of the first class and therefore it is logical to expect that the latter's masts would have been just that much larger.

The three masts on a Chinese junk were not positioned in a single straight line as in Western ships, but staggered. They also did not rise vertically but were raked at different angles. This gave the junk a rather crank appearance but was in some ways a better distribution of weight, particularly when one considers that a ship is not a stable platform but continually rolling and pitching. The Chinese were also far less concerned about the mast being perfectly straight than were their Western counterparts, regarding a bend in a spar as a sign of strength.

The depth of the hold of the *Keying* was about sixteen feet (5m) and it was divided transversely into approximately fifteen different sections by means of watertight bulkheads. It was also divided longitudinally at intervals of about four to five feet (1.2–1.5m). The use of watertight bulkheads had been common among the Chinese since the time of Marco Polo, who commented:

Some ships, namely those which are larger, have besides quite thirteen holds, that is divisions on the inside, made with strong planks fitted together, so that if by accident the ship is staved in any place ... the sailors find out where the ship is staved, and then the hold which answers to the break is emptied into others, for the water cannot pass from one hold to another, so strongly are they shut in; and then they repair the ship there, and put back there the goods which had been taken out.

The *Tek Sing* wreck shows similar evidence of transverse and longitudinal bulkheads.

One of the most startling differences between Western and Eastern ships was the Chinese rudder. On Western ships the rudder was fixed and hinged on a system of gudgeons and pintles. On the junk the rudder was balanced in a kind of slot at the stern of the ship and could be raised or lowered by means of two great bamboo cables that went right under the bottom of the hull. The rudder on the *Keying* weighed about eight ton(ne)s and required at least fifteen men to raise and lower it, and in times of heavy weather twenty men might be required to control the tiller. The advantage of having a rudder that could be moved vertically was that it could be brought in board when the ship was sailing through sandy or shoal water, but in mid-ocean it could be lowered, increasing the draught of the ship to some twenty-four feet (7.3m), giving it a greater hold in the water and enabling it to sail closer to the wind. If the *Tek Sing*'s rudder was in the lowered position when it struck the

A stack of woks on the sea-bed. *(Dave Moran)*

Right: A painting of the Keying. *(Chinese School, c. 1850, Martyn Gregory Gallery, London.)*

An interesting view of the Tek Sing*'s timber framework, with some original rope, made from bamboo fibre, still in near-perfect condition. (Dave Moran)*

Mike Hatcher celebrates after another hard day of recovery work. (Ocean Salvage Corporation)

Belvidere, as seems highly probable since the pilot clearly thought that he was sailing in open seas, it would have given those on board the most tremendous jolt. Interestingly, the historical accounts do refer to the intensity of that first impact. The rudder would have acted like a hook, catching on the ledge of rock and probably holding the junk on the reef for the first hour until the bottom of the hull was ripped out. From this point the *Tek Sing* beat over the reef and floundered southwards for a little over a kilometre before precipitously sinking. No evidence has yet been found of the rudder in the general debris of the wreck but it is quite possible that it became detached from the ship and lies at some distance from the main hull, closer to the reef. It is hoped that further excavation at the site will disclose its remains. It would be interesting to know whether it was perforated in the same manner as the rudder of the *Keying*. The exact purpose of these perforations is not entirely understood but it is thought that they were intended to make the rudder lighter in weight; at eight tonnes it was certainly quite heavy enough. The perforations would also have made the rudder easier to move through the water when a change of direction was required. If the tiller required twenty men to move it during times of heavy weather, it would have presumably required even more hands if the rudder had not been perforated.

Unfortunately, just as Captain Pearl's venture in 1822 was overtaken by political events in Borneo

124

between the Dutch and the Chinese, so, nearly two hundred years later, Mike Hatcher's somewhat different venture was abruptly interrupted by the rapidly deteriorating political situation in Indonesia. By October 1999 the troubles in East Timor, which had brought the *Restless M* to the Gelasa Straits in the first place, looked like engulfing the entire region. Australians, in particular, because of their peace-keeping role on East Timor, became a target for hard-line Indonesian nationalists. The personnel of Ocean Salvage Corporation found themselves having to leave Jakarta in a hurry, crouched on the floors of taxis in order to avoid stray bullets. Mike Hatcher, stuck out in the middle of the Gelasa Straits, was particularly vulnerable to some wayward attack by a group of lawless insurgents, even though the salvage operation had at all times been conducted in accordance with a licence issued by the Indonesian Government. At sea, in this particular area of the globe, which is still today infested with pirates, pieces of paper don't always count for that much. The barrel of a gun is – all too often – the more decisive factor in determining outcomes. With the threat of a total breakdown of law and order, Stephen McNamara, the managing director of Ocean Salvage, in conjunction with Mike, decided it would be best to bring the operation to a premature close rather than risk an incident that could cause loss of life. If, however, the opportunity should ever arise, much more can certainly be learned from this unique wreck site.

Mike Hatcher and crew member at sundown. (Dave Moran)

Amoy

PART THREE

THE PORCELAIN
on the
TEK SING

The Porcelain

CHINESE CERAMICS HAVE A LONG and glorious history dating back more than five thousand years. Best known from this early period are pots of simple form with painted geometric motifs, fired in simple kilns to a relatively low temperature. Already by about 1300 BC there appeared a major development in production, that of glazing, allowing vessels to be impermeable for the first time. By the Han dynasty, just around the start of the Christian era, hard-bodied, high-fired ceramics had taken a firm hold. At this time, glazes were generally green or to a lesser extent amber, and most pieces were monochrome. Any pictorial motifs on glazed vases were incised into the body of a piece or produced from a mould.

Over the ensuing centuries techniques developed substantially, and in Tang times (AD 618–906) one finds a wonderful variety of forms, both vessels and tomb figures, covered in often dramatic glazes, either monochrome or any combination of green, amber, straw-colour and blue. Perhaps the most famous products of the period – indeed of Chinese ceramics of any age – are the Tang horse and camel, buried with the deceased to accompany them into the afterlife, objects beloved of several generations of collectors. The dramatic, bright colours of the Tang gave way in the tenth century to the more restrained glazes of the Song dynasty (960–1277). It was around this period

Previous pages: A view of Amoy after the first Opium War. Amoy had been a major port for the export of porcelain to the wider Asian market for many centuries, but the junk trade declined after the close of the Opium Wars. (Chinese artist, c. 1850, Martyn Gregory Gallery, London.)

Left: One of a series of paintings depicting the various stages of porcelain manufacture. This shows the packing of the porcelain in large tubs. (Chinese School, early 19th century, Christie's Images Ltd, London.)

129

that another major breakthrough in ceramic production was developing: the application of a high-fired, hard vitreous material. This, through the mixing of two locally available materials, kaolin and petuntse, allowed the applied glaze to fuse to the body of the piece. This eventually became known as porcelain and in the early days of its export, by diffusion as well as by travellers' reports, it became one of the wonders of the world.

By the Yuan period (1277–1368) the production centre of Jingdezhen was well established as perhaps the most important in China. It was at this time that something of a cottage industry became industrialised under government supervision. This was largely due to the popularity of these high-fired, porcellaneous wares among foreign traders from the Song dynasty onwards. By the late sixteenth century, what began as a trickle became a veritable flood of Jingdezhen goods to Europe. Not for want of trying, it was not until the eighteenth century, however, that the ceramic factories of Europe managed to devise a process that gave a product with the same qualities. In the meantime the magical substance from the mysterious Orient became known as 'china'.

A major development in Yuan times was the new decorative technique of painting the body of a piece in blue (or, much less often, red) and then applying a colourless glaze. It was a major innovation, since hitherto (with rare exceptions) only incising or moulding could produce pictorial motifs. Not long after, in the Ming dynasty (1368–1644), overglaze enamels of various colours were introduced by experimentation with numerous chemicals, and by the eighteenth century these had become highly sophisticated.

Industrialisation of Jingdezhen made it the main centre not only of exportwares to many areas of the world, but also of items for the home market, most notably pieces for the emperor himself. The high degree of specialisation ensured the highest quality in every domain of production when this was required, although quality over the centuries was to some extent a function of such outside influences as political climate or the public purse. The highest standards during the Ming and Qing (1644–1911) periods were not applied very often to exportwares, and it would appear that the producers responded differently to the demands of the various markets that they were serving. As a general but by no means infallible rule, Europe-bound merchandise seems to have been of a higher quality than that made for places such as the East Indies or India. However, the best for all destinations could be of a remarkable fineness, clearly acknowledging a class system in the purchasing communities.

In the later periods quality of production peaked in the reign of Yongzheng (1723–35) and started a decline towards the end of the eighteenth century in the reign of Qianlong (1736–95). At this time, exports to Europe were being interrupted. The Napoleonic Wars caused disruption while production at Jingdezhen

Right: Unusually large glazed pottery model of a camel from the Tang dynasty (618–906), buried with the deceased to serve in the afterlife. Note the vessels on the saddle-cloth, which are exact replicas of life-sized ones also found in tombs. (S. Marchant & Son, London.)

130

was in decline, both numerically and qualitatively, partly because demand in Europe was also diminishing since at long last the big factories had discovered a formula for producing wares of similar appearance, hardness and durability.

Throughout the time that porcelain was being produced at mainstream Jingdezhen in Jiangsi province, there was a thriving area of production in neighbouring Fujian province to the south, centred upon the town of Dehua. Already in neolithic times, according to the archaeological record, there was ceramic production and by Song and Yuan times it was being exported overseas. Numerous natural features of the province favoured the development of a flourishing ceramic industry. First and foremost was the presence in abundance of kaolin, a principal raw material of porcelain production. Much of the area being wooded and mountainous, there was plenty of fuel for the kilns and fast-flowing water to turn the water-wheels – a common feature of the landscape until fairly recently – that operated the machinery for processing the kaolin. Furthermore, communication by river from Dehua to the ports of Fuzhou and Quanzhou was relatively easy. In the nineteenth century Xiamen (Amoy) was also an important port for export. Thus there was good communication not only internally but also to the foreign markets.

It would appear from archaeological finds that most producers were working on a small scale, perhaps in families, and that many did not own their own kilns, but took their wares to kiln-owners for firing. Eventually goods were assembled in various market-towns for shipment beyond. Rare sets of twelve rice-paper paintings show the process of production. The first three pictures show digging, breaking and pounding the clay; the next two show the turning or shaping of pots; then comes glazing followed by a first firing; then decoration and a second firing; the wares are hauled over mountains to a central distribution point for packing; next is a shop and finally a packing area for export.

It is from this production area – and possibly some little way beyond – that the bulk of the *Tek Sing*'s cargo came. Judging by the style and quality of the wares, most if not all was destined for places further south and east. It is reasonable to assume that little if any of the output would have been destined for Europe, since it was of a style unlikely to have found favour with Western merchants and their public. This is borne out by the fact that very little of this merchandise is extant in Europe today. In any case, as mentioned above, by now Europe was producing its own porcelain and did not need to import wares made expensive by transport costs and risks.

Almost the entire Fujian cargo is utilitarian, objects of everyday use, mostly bowls, plates, dishes and boxes of varying dimensions. Because of the softness of the kaolin in Fujian, pieces usually had thick bodies in order to avoid breakage in manufacture. By far the largest part is blue and white but there are also a relatively small number of white wares, some with moulded decoration and some plain.

In presenting an overview of the items from Fujian on board, it is perhaps appropriate to start with these latter. This is because in its heyday of fine production in the late sixteenth, seventeenth and early eighteenth centuries, Dehua was producing large amounts of white wares, known in the West as *blanc de Chine*. These were almost invariably of high quality, taking the forms of libation cups, vessels and figure groups, items of a ritual or amusing nature. Although white utilitarian items were undoubtedly produced in numbers, such as boxes very similar to those in the cargo, the emphasis of the better-quality wares appears to have been more religio-decorative, largely for the domestic market, although they found an enthusiastic market in Europe. The best figures were sometimes signed by the potters and are much sought after to this day. The esteem in which *blanc de Chine* was held is illustrated by the fact that a beaker-vase of the type was found in the tomb of the Emperor Wanli, who died in 1619.

As far as dating the objects on board is concerned, very little is known about the age of Fujian and other South Chinese wares. It does, however, seem reasonable to assume that those pieces present in very large numbers were new at the time of shipment. This is not an infallible rule, as will be seen below, but it is unlikely that in the many cases in this cargo where there are hundreds or even thousands of similar items, they would have been stored for some decades or longer and then suddenly come to light.

If we begin by examining the white circular boxes, it has to be conceded that the larger ones hardly differ, if at all, from those found in the *Vung Tao* cargo, salvaged some years ago and dating from the 1690s. It would be unrealistic to think of the present examples as surfacing after 130 years and one should conclude that a conservative community of potters continued a successful line with no reason to

White boxes with moulded peony and leaf designs, the larger examples following a long tradition going back at least 120 years. (Nagel Auctions, Stuttgart.)

White bowls of simple, elegant form, present in large numbers in the cargo. (Nagel Auctions, Stuttgart.)

abandon it. Indeed, boxes not too dissimilar are known from two or three centuries earlier than the *Vung Tao* examples. The delightful, moulded flowering peony on the cover is a typical motif, rather more common than the leaf on the smaller boxes of similar type.

Other white wares in the cargo are relatively few, perhaps surprisingly when one considers that it is for its earlier white wares that Dehua is famous today. Indeed, one of the great enigmas has been the sudden apparent near-disappearance of *blanc de Chine* after about 1730 until its re-emergence in much more recent times. Here, there are three types of winecup, one shallow with an elegant flared side – so delicate that one is tempted to question whether it is germane to its more sturdy Dehua counterparts. Of these one is deeper and narrower, the other as shallow but with a rounded side. There are also a large number of rice-bowls with elegant flared sides. Finally, one should note the white spoons, again similar to but slightly less ornate than those in the *Vung Tao* cargo. They are partnered by some blue-and-white ones with floral designs and a very interesting group of brown-glazed ones. Brown-glazed Dehua wares were certainly made at the end of the seventeenth century but were very rare. The present ones seem to be a re-invention or continuation of the type.

Very similar in form, glaze and body to the white boxes are the ones with covers decorated in underglaze-blue. These also come in two sizes. The larger have very artistic free designs showing many subjects including carp, shrimp, aster, chrysanthemum and peony flowerheads and even love poems. The smaller boxes have simpler but equally attractive and free-flowing designs. A much smaller group of

Left: Rare white and brown spoons from Fujian, the white ones reminiscent of similar spoons in the Vung Tao *cargo dating to c. 1690. (Nagel Auctions, Stuttgart.)*

Below: Boxes, painted with numerous different charming designs executed with a fine and elegant hand. (Nagel Auctions, Stuttgart.)

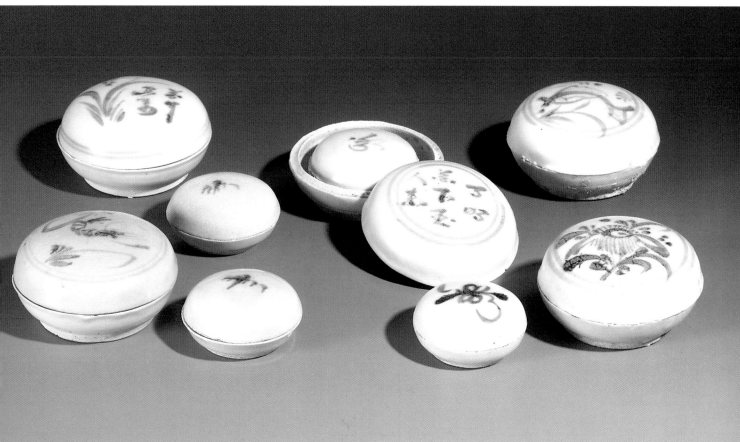

Above: Boxes with peony and landscape designs, the matching small ones fitting perfectly into the larger ones. (Nagel Auctions, Stuttgart.)

One of a small group of hexagonal boxes painted with linear floral motifs. They are virtually the only angular pieces in the cargo. (Nagel Auctions, Stuttgart.)

boxes with straight instead of rounded sides are painted with either landscapes or floral motifs. Their particular charm is that the smaller box fits so snugly into the larger that they were put one inside the other not just to save room in transport but because they were meant to be marketed as a set. Another type, hexagonal with a linear floral motif and virtually the only angular pieces in the cargo, makes up the complement of boxes.

Apart from the white winecups, several other varieties are evident in numbers in the cargo. Probably most numerous are those of conical form with fungus and peach motif (discussed below), which type has been found on various Fujian kiln-sites. They are pleasing of form and the motifs, though sketchy, are by a trained hand. Of closely similar form are those decorated with two bands of vertical linear patterns. These are of especial interest in that it is almost certain that this motif was applied not with the brush but by block printing. Careful observation suggests that each individual unit of design is an exact replica – bar the inevitable unevenness of the colour application – of its neighbour. As far as I am aware, this technique was never employed at Jingdezhen. Among the remaining types is an unusual blue-and-white winecup of slightly more elegant form with the side more rounded towards the base and a design of white dots and dashes showing through a wide blue band. This so-called reverse technique requires much skill. A charming feature is its disproportionately wide

A selection of crackled celadon pieces found in small numbers in the cargo. (Nagel Auctions, Stuttgart.)

unglazed area of footrim, reminiscent of those on Jingdezhen pieces of the early Kangxi (1662–1722) and Yongzheng (1723–35) periods.

Finally, mention should be made of a group of pale crackled celadon winecups of shallow, rounded form, which with their delicate footrim and wall of tapering thickness towards the rim have a refinement that may suggest a different place of origin. Other similarly crackled celadon pieces in the cargo, however, appear to have southern origins.

It is of course unsurprising that a cargo should be largely utilitarian in content, thus comprising a preponderance of bowls and dishes. Among the most noteworthy are the bowls and dishes of various dimensions with the design of fungus and peach (sometimes a flowerhead), similar to but more elaborate than the winecups already mentioned. It is more than likely that this design has its origins in Jingdezhen, which had produced designs in the previous centuries of bowls, dishes and even boxes whose motifs were, as with these, placed within petal-shaped panels, which in their totality form a flowerhead. Many pieces have an added attraction of a beautifully applied spiral centre.

A group of white and celadon miniature vases, offering a variety of interesting shapes and decorations. (Nagel Auctions, Stuttgart.)

Probably the majority of Chinese motifs, be they plant, animal or figural, have auspicious meanings. Whether the Fujian potters had these in mind as they planned their next production is not known, but it is plausible that subjects with particular

auspicious significance might help sales to a generally superstitious public. Certainly the high-quality wares made in Jingdezhen for the Emperor often had all the motifs on a piece symbolising one or possibly more themes, be they long life, many descendants, happiness or wealth etc. In the case of the fungus and peach motif, longevity is the theme, so that these bowls and dishes have gained the epithet 'birthday'. The flowerhead itself, though unidentifiable, is probably the lotus. This also symbolises long life, thus keeping the unity of the theme.

A large number of dishes and a lesser quantity of bowls have the very traditional motif of flowering plants issuing from or beside rocks. The large quantity on board suggests that this was popular with customers and although the quality of most has a certain eccentric naïvety, it is this that gives the pieces their charm. The majority of the dishes have peony (wealth, rank) and magnolia (purity) each side of a central rock; however, a small number have just prunus (perseverance, purity) and yet others have bamboo (humility and fidelity), peony and reeds issuing from rocks. A small number have magnolia and peony but no rocks.

Of the remaining blue-and-white flatwares, suffice it to mention the following briefly. The small plates with a basket of unidentifiable flowers in the centre have a design rooted in the Ming dynasty; early eighteenth-century Jingdezhen blue-and-white plates with this subject have the same unusual blue-wash border. Also echoing eighteenth-century Jingdezhen are the two flatwares with flowerhead designs.

One of the predominant patterns in the cargo. The bowls and dishes themselves are in the form of a bloom and each petal encloses a lingzhi-fungus, peach or flowerhead, symbols of longevity. (Nagel Auctions, Stuttgart.)

139

Top left: Rice-bowls and covers with peony design, in very small numbers in the cargo. (Nagel Auctions, Stuttgart.)

Centre left: A group of items with peony and magnolia design. (Nagel Auctions, Stuttgart.)

Bottom left: Traditional Chinese motifs, various plants around and issuing from central rockwork including bamboo, peony, reeds and prunus. (Nagel Auctions, Stuttgart.)

Left: A 19th-century South Chinese version of the time-honoured design depicting a central basket of flowers. (Nagel Auctions, Stuttgart.)

Particularly attractive are the dishes with a chrysanthemum flowerhead (longevity) surrounded by sprays of finger-citron, pomegranate (fecundity) and peach. The plates have a peony flowerhead with foliage within two narrow formal bands. Of particular charm for the finesse of execution of the designs are the simple small dishes with characters or flowers, similar in feeling to the designs on the boxes of like size.

Finally, there are the lovely dishes with water-reeds emerging from water in which flowering plants are growing. The best of the group are reminiscent, in the rendering of the grasses with free and elegant brushstrokes, of the wonderful Jingdezhen blue-and-white pieces with similar motifs from the 1690s. The poem also on each dish speaks of a clear freshwater spring in the moonlight beneath the clouds.

The bowls offer a large variety of subjects and forms. Certainly most dramatic and probably most interesting are the large ones with a design in two rows of alternating stylised *shou* (longevity) characters and a complex device, possibly floral. What is

Above left: One of the few groups of plates with flattened rims. The peony motif was much favoured in the 18th century and its popularity continued into *the next century. (Nagel Auctions, Stuttgart.)*
Left: Charming small dishes painted with an elegant, free hand with characters and flowers. (Nagel Auctions, Stuttgart.)

Above: Three saucer dishes typical of the cargo and probably emanating from the same factory. The first two show chrysanthemums; the third water-reeds painted with *a particular refinement. (Nagel Auctions, Stuttgart.)*
Below: Imposing large bowls decorated with the unusual technique of block printing. (Nagel Auctions, Stuttgart.)

especially interesting is again the use of a block-print process, which is evident on smaller bowls with the same *shou* character. At least three other types of bowl use the same technique, one with chrysanthemum flowerheads, one with a band of peony and magnolia, and the large shallow bowls with two geometric bands around the unglazed centre, which sometimes has a stamped maker's or owner's mark or just one of commendation. It is indeed a feature of many Fujian pieces in this cargo that they are stamped in this way or marked calligraphically.

Other blue-and-white bowls in the cargo have various floral motifs, more or less similar to the dishes already mentioned. One exception is the group of bowls with a circle and dot motif, whose simplicity gives them their charm. Lastly must be mentioned the bowls depicting a figure standing by a fence. Together with a group of dishes with a delightful scene of a man in a terraced garden seated at a table with two incense burners on it, and another with a figure standing on a terrace (scenes typical of Jingdezhen porcelain in the second half of the seventeenth century), these represent almost the only figural scenes in the whole cargo. Judging by the illustration of sherds excavated at various Dehua sites, shown by Jianzhong Chen in *Dehua Folk Blue and White Wares*, this proportion may well mirror the general output. Perhaps worthy of mention as an appendage to the figural items is a single dish with an insect in the centre, certainly a charming and unusual subject.

Other blue-and-white articles of a utilitarian nature are the few urinals with floral and landscape decoration. Urinals of various forms are known from Jingdezhen from the seventeenth and eighteenth centuries and it is possible, but unlikely, that these were produced there rather than in Fujian. There was in the cargo a small quantity

Above: Dishes with two charming designs reminiscent of those on porcelains of the 17th century from Jingdezhen. (Nagel Auctions, Stuttgart.)

Top left: Bowls decorated with floral motifs and shou *(long life) characters with a block-printing technique. (Nagel Auctions, Stuttgart.)*

Centre left: Bowls with landscape design. The similarities of the elements of the decoration suggest block printing. (Nagel Auctions, Stuttgart.)

Bottom left: Group of bowls with a design of a boy on a terrace reaching out to a butterfly; and another of a scholar on a terrace. (Nagel Auctions, Stuttgart.)

Two of about ten unusual urinals (possibly water-vessels) in the cargo. One has bamboo decoration, the other a landscape. Other motifs are floral. Urinals in Chinese porcelain go back at least to the 17th century. (Nagel Auctions, Stuttgart.)

with red bodies, which may have come from the Yixing region in nearby Jiangsu province.

It is from Yixing and the surrounding area that the relatively small number of typically red-bodied items on the ship come. As in the Dehua area, ceramic production goes back millennia. Sherds five thousand years old have been excavated. The area was similarly favoured with good, relatively easily obtainable raw materials, and numerous waterways enabled efficient distribution. Much of the output was of less refined quality, made for local use or export to nearby lands. A small number of jars – ovoid, conical and of other forms – were salvaged, differing in size from very large to tableware dimensions. These were accompanied by a few very rare small, thickly potted stoves, some red-bodied.

It was during the relatively peaceful Ming times that this fertile area gave rise to a rich and cultured elite

Above: Red-bodied urinal (possibly a water-vessel) similar in form to those on the previous page. (Nagel Auctions, Stuttgart.)

Large kettle with moulded dragon design. Only a small number of this remarkable type, almost all different from the next, were in the cargo. (Nagel Auctions, Stuttgart.)

147

Three of a small number of pottery stoves, two with a lower chamber for fuel below a perforated shelf and one with a drawer for fuel. (Nagel Auctions, Stuttgart.)

A selection of thin-bodied, olive-glazed vessels of delicate potting. Note the delightful fish-shaped knops on the covers. (Nagel Auctions, Stuttgart.)

society, one of whose traditions was the taking of tea. These merchants, officials and scholars as well as aristocrats required the finest tea and by the sixteenth century there was a great appreciation of the red-bodied teapots produced at Yixing. It became a matter not only of pleasure but also of status to order – or indeed sometimes to help the potter to produce – the finest possible teapots. In Ming times and later, inscriptions were of great importance. They could be extracts from poems of earlier origin or modern, and in some cases the simple but elegant forms of the

vessels were no more than vehicles for fine calligraphy. The tea-drinkers of Jiangsu and Zhejiang provinces eschewed what they deemed the more gaudy decorative products of Jingdezhen and the gold and silver pots favoured in some quarters. On the practical side, these unglazed pots kept the tea warm for longer, retained aroma better and were usually small enough to help avoid wasting an expensive commodity. The eighteenth century saw a decline in interest in and quality of Yixing teapots but there was a revival at the start of the nineteenth century, though earlier heights were never again reached.

All the teapots from the cargo have the traditional elegant simplicity of these wares. Some of the shapes have the maker's name and others have poetic inscriptions on their bases. While there is a long history of exporting Yixing teapots, it is perhaps surprising to find inscribed ones in the cargo. Presumably they were destined for some of the island emigrant Chinese communities, where such cultural objects would be appreciated among certain classes. It is interesting that one of the Yixing teapots recovered from the Nanking cargo, salvaged in 1985 and whose wares date from circa 1750, appears very similar to the bullet-shaped teapots in the present cargo. Given the small number, it is not impossible that the latter were 'old stock' recovered from some warehouse, but it is more likely that some of the older types continued to be made alongside newer, more refined versions that were part of the revival.

Another area of production represented is Swatow, in the southern province of Guandong. There are a number of large blue-glazed dishes and some coloured bowls with matching underdishes. These are virtually the only pieces in the cargo painted with overglaze colours, namely yellow, green and iron red. One type offers a

A selection of very finely made red-bodied Yixing teapots. Famous for their simple forms, they often bear poetic inscriptions, two of which are shown below. (Nagel Auctions, Stuttgart.)

149

Part of a group of some hundreds of delightful boys salvaged. This type intriguingly dates from about 1750 and its presence on board is something of an enigma. (Nagel Auctions, Stuttgart.)

charming rendering of a lotus bloom, petals on the exterior and the pod in the well of the interior. Another type displays a band of flowers alternating with trellis above lotus petals.

The origins of a certain number of pieces cannot be identified with certainty, although it is reasonable to assume that they are from the above-mentioned areas or

Two charming and very rare models of ducks with hooks for hanging. (Nagel Auctions, Stuttgart.)

nearby. Most striking perhaps are the large kettles with relief dragon motifs. Then there are the light-bodied pouring vessels similar to others in the *Diana* cargo, and the various olive-glazed items – carafes and bowls and covers of various dimensions, the largest having an incised floral design, others with charming fish or Budai (god of happiness) knops. All are finely made and, following time-honoured Chinese tradition, the glaze of many runs down unevenly, stopping short of the foot. Then there is a group of very rare near-spherical lightweight objects with slightly conical protrusions, which were used to hold opium. All are finely incised and appear once to have been thinly glazed. Also of note are a number of mostly grey-bodied, large storage jars, some glazed, some with incised decoration and others plain.

Finally, there are a number of items that do not fit the utilitarian nature of the overwhelming mass of the cargo. Of these many definitely date from earlier periods. Of particular significance is the group of seated boys of extremely high quality, poorer versions of which figured in the Nanking cargo. They undoubtedly come from Jingdezhen. What is somewhat baffling is that they date from about 1750; such quality in figure production is not found much later, so that they cannot be a continued line. One may assume that given the numbers on board they were trading goods and not simply the personal belongings of a passenger. They must have turned up in some hidden corner of a warehouse. In whichever case, they were never put in the cargo hold and were found stored in jars. Clearly their owner held them in high esteem. Other figure models are the ducks and reclining dogs.

Pair of charming reclining dogs, very similar in feeling to coloured examples being made at the same time in Jingdezhen. (Nagel Auctions, Stuttgart.)

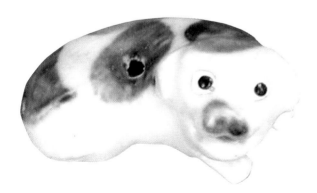

Two remarkable models of birds found in very small numbers in the cargo. They have holes in their bases but their exact function is unclear. (Nagel Auctions, Stuttgart.)

The latter are so reminiscent of Jingdezhen models with coloured enamels of the 1820s and 1830s that these may possibly hail from there. Other decorative objects are the brown and buff sparrow-like models, whose origin is unclear. Given their delicacy, they may be from Yixing, whose tradition it was in later times to decorate some of the more elaborate teapots with applied ceramic objects copying nature, in hues from dark brown to white. Of note also are a number of glazed roosters, very similar to those on the *Diana*, a ship that went down in 1817.

A few other objects are earlier in date than the bulk of the cargo. The types are so few in number that they may be deemed to be passengers' personal belongings.

An amusing group of roosters, very similar to those found in the cargo of the Diana, *which went down in 1817. (Nagel Auctions, Stuttgart.)*

There are an eighteenth-century *flambé* vase from Jingdezhen, a few Ming tripod celadon censers from Zhejiang province and a Jingdezhen shallow blue-and-white censer on five bracket feet with lotus and chrysanthemum flowerheads and scrolling foliage, dating to the end of the eighteenth century. Lastly, there is an intriguing white vase of square shape, the only non-utilitarian white piece in the cargo and by appearance of the high-quality *blanc de Chine*, probably of earlier date, though owing to weathering it is hard to know. Obviously, with these individual items, one cannot be sure whether there are others in sherds on the sea-bed.

In conclusion, this remarkable cargo breaks new ground in the history of salvage. Not only is it by far the largest to date, but it also contains a significant variety of southern Chinese wares not included in the previous cargoes. With future research into its contents, useful information may be obtained on trading patterns and ceramic types. From the collector's point of view, there will never be a better opportunity to obtain some of these often rare porcelains unfamiliar to Westerners, with their great charm and many eccentricities.

Above: White-glazed vase in the form of an archaic jade vessel. This could be a 17th-century piece of fine blanc de Chine, *a personal possession of someone on board. (Nagel Auctions, Stuttgart.)*

One of a handful of early Ming celadon incense burners dating from the early 15th century, surely a treasured possession of one of the passengers. (Nagel Auctions, Stuttgart.)

PART FOUR

FROM ZHENG HE
to the
OPIUM WARS

From Zheng He to the Opium Wars

THE ROOTS OF CHINESE maritime exploration and trading stretch back to before the birth of Christ. In the period of the Tang dynasty, commencing in AD 618, it is evident that Chinese commercial networks stretched westwards as far as East Africa, Persia and India. It is unlikely that Chinese junks were themselves voyaging across the Indian Ocean during the Tang period, or the Sung period which followed. Instead there would have been an exchange of valued commodities, such as exotic animals and medicinal drugs, through intermediaries such as Arab seafarers utilising entrepôt ports like Calicut. One such, Ibn Battutah, writing in 1342, referred to 13 Chinese junks being in the port of Calicut when he visited it. By the time of the Ming Emperor Zhu Di, in the early fifteenth century, China had become indisputably the world's dominant maritime power. The famed Zheng He treasure ships were by then penetrating directly as far afield as Malindi and Mogadishu on the East African coast, Aden and Mecca in the Middle East, and Bengal in India.

Zheng He was the Chinese Grand Eunuch, famed for his military prowess, and appointed by Zhu Di as overall commander of the seven great expeditions into the Indian Ocean, which took place between 1405 and 1433. These expeditions were a colossal naval undertaking, each one involving over sixty of the great

Previous pages: Hong Kong by a Chinese artist, shortly after the close of the first Opium War, showing a mixture of Chinese and Western shipping. Lord Palmerston regarded Hong Kong as a barren island and the least significant prize of the war. (Martyn Gregory Gallery, London.)

Left: The Nemesis attacking Chinese junks on the Pearl River in January 1841. (Painted by G.W. Terry, National Maritime Museum, London.)

treasure ships, and several hundred supply boats and support craft. In total nearly thirty thousand men were mustered for each voyage. The personnel included not just sailors and soldiers, but also diplomats, astrologers, doctors, interpreters, accountants, business factors, and all manner of specialist craftsmen. Some 37 countries were visited, each expedition lasting approximately two years. The purposes of these ambitious voyages – which predate the activities of Columbus and Vasco da Gama and make the latter look somewhat amateurish by comparison – were various and complex. The main aim was to exact tribute from all those countries that China considered to be its vassals (in effect, all other countries in their contingent world), and ruthlessly to suppress any dissidents. To this end the notorious Palembang pirate Ch'en Tsu-I was defeated and brought back to Nanking for execution on the first expedition, and rebels in the island of Ceylon were destroyed on the third. As well as having a military function, however, there was also a trading purpose. The holds of the treasure ships were full of prized blue-and-white and celadon porcelains, rich silks, lacquer ware, art objects and devotional statues. The merchants on board were eager to acquire ivory, elephants, parakeets, pearls, precious stones, rhinoceros horns, incense, spices, horses and innumerable other highly valued items. It was this cargo that led to the term 'treasure ships' being used by the Chinese themselves. The voyages were also an expression of a serious search for new knowledge. The scientists

This rather dramatised view of the iniquities of a Chinese opium den, by the British artist Thomas Allom, contrasts with the rather more mundane portrayals of the vice by Chinese artists of the same period. (University Library, Cambridge.)

on board were instructed to bring back rare plants, minerals and gems as well as an exotic collection of little-known animals such as giraffes, lions, leopards, zebras and camels – all for the purpose of further study as well as courtly amusement. On a more personal level, it has been suggested that the Emperor Zhu Di, whose health was failing, was anxiously in search of new medicinal drugs.

The size and structure of the treasure ships has been the subject of much learned debate throughout several centuries of scholarship. Chinese sources suggest that the larger ships were over 130 metres long and 55 metres wide with nine masts and a burthen in excess of 3,000 tonnes. Some commentators have cast doubt on these figures, suggesting that a wooden ship of such proportions would be inherently unstable. However, the recent discovery of a huge rudder near Nanking, dating back to the Zheng He period, with a blade area of 42 square metres has led some naval architects to argue that this would imply a ship of the size stated in the ancient Chinese sources. Certainly the treasure ships had some four decks raised above the main deck, as well as further decks below, providing relatively spacious living quarters for the more important dignitaries. Ibn Battutah, reporting on Chinese trading junks approximately one hundred years before the Zheng He period, comments on their large size:

A Chinese prince, c. 1800, by a Chinese artist. The Manchu court remained hopelessly out of touch with political and military realities throughout the war and afterwards. (Martyn Gregory Gallery, London.)

In the vessel they build four decks, and it has cabins, suites and salons for merchants; a set of rooms has several rooms and a latrine; it can be locked by an occupant and he can take along with him slave-girls and wives. Often a man will live in his suite unknown to any of the others on board until they meet on reaching some town. The sailors have their children living on board ship and they cultivate green stuffs, vegetables and ginger in wooden tanks ...There is no people in the world wealthier than the Chinese.

But Chinese naval supremacy did not last for very long. Soon after the death of Zhu Di, China turned its back on the world and, in the spirit of Confucian scholasticism, closed its doors to foreign trade. It was left to the Portuguese and the Spanish to control the world's trade routes, to be followed one hundred years later by the Dutch and the British.

If the period of the Zheng He treasure ships witnessed the zenith of Chinese maritime power, the period of the Opium Wars demonstrated a devastating decline. Throughout the 1820s and 1830s, relations between Britain and China steadily deteriorated. The Chinese issued more edicts against opium smuggling, made more arrests of Chinese merchants suspected of acting as intermediaries in the drug distribution networks, and introduced harsher sentencing. But the drug continued to flood in.

In 1729, it has been estimated, about 200 chests of opium were imported into China. By the 1820s this number had grown to 10,000 chests annually. By the middle of the nineteenth century, after the conclusion of the Opium Wars, consumption had escalated still further to around 70,000 chests.

The British, American and European dealers were entirely deaf to the moral arguments in favour of prohibition. Opium was a legal commodity in the rest of the world, so why not in China? Prohibition was contrary to the fundamental and overriding liberal principle of free trade. The problem was not with opium itself, so the argument went, but within the Chinese character. They were a morally depraved people susceptible to addiction. If the Chinese were serious about solving their opium problem, they needed to put their own house in order. The view held generally was similar to that of John Trotter, who oversaw opium production in Benares: 'I never knew one solitary instance of impaired health amongst natives resulting from the use of the drug, not even in the factories, where people passed twelve hours a day in an opium atmosphere and ate as much as they could consume.' And anyway – according to popular opinion among the British – it was not opium addicts that the Chinese were really worried about. It was the loss of silver that was upsetting them. There were those in the West who argued against the trade, such as A.S. Thelwell, who published a book called *The Iniquities of the Opium Trade*. But these arguments did not carry much weight with the big shipping companies in Canton, like Dents, or Jardine Matheson.

Matters came to a head at the beginning of 1839 when Emperor Dao Guang appointed Commissioner Lin Tse-Hsu, with special responsibility to stamp out the opium trade once and for all. Commissioner Lin was a typical poet-scholar of the mandarin class. But unlike so many of his predecessors, he was not prepared to turn an expediently blind eye to what was going on under his nose. He demanded that all the opium at present in Canton and on the Pearl River be handed over forthwith.

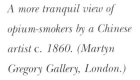

A more tranquil view of opium-smokers by a Chinese artist c. 1860. (Martyn Gregory Gallery, London.)

When the merchants (predictably) refused to comply, Lin took the unprecedented step of barricading the suspected ringleaders inside the English factory, thus putting them under virtual house arrest. Eventually, the Superintendent of Trade, Charles Elliot, defused the immediate crisis by organising the surrender of 20,000 chests of opium, which quantity gives some idea of the scale of the drug problem at the time. He was only able to get the merchants to comply with this hand-over by privately promising them indemnity for their losses from the British Government. Meanwhile he sent off an urgent dispatch to the British Governor-General in Calcutta for naval reinforcements.

Commissioner Lin took possession of the 20,000 chests and housed them in a special compound. The opium cakes were broken open and the liquid run off into the Pearl River. He prayed to Tianfei to tell the ocean creatures to move away to avoid being poisoned. He believed, like many in China, that opium was produced by the 'foreign devils' from crows that had been allowed to feed on human corpses. The stench of the opium drifted across the entire town and thousands of onlookers came to see what was happening.

Then the temperature was raised by the murder of a Chinese citizen, Lin Wei-Hsi, by a gang of British and American sailors. The Chinese – as usual – insisted on the murderer being handed over for trial according to Chinese law. The captain of the ship involved – as usual – refused. Essentially what the British were claiming here was a legal right to extraterritoriality. It was not that Chinese law was particularly harsh – indeed, in many ways, compared with British law of the time, it was relatively

Opium-receiving ships at the island of Lintin in the Pearl River, 1824. At times when smuggling opium directly into Whampoa or Macao was too difficult, the Western traders would transfer their chests of opium into old hulks, called receiving ships, moored outside the official area of Chinese jurisdiction. From there the opium would be collected by fast Chinese oared boats called 'fast crabs' or 'scrambling dragons'. (Painted by William Huggins, National Maritime Museum, London.)

merciful. However, it did sanction torture as a means of obtaining a confession and it had no concept of trial by jury. For the British this was simply unacceptable. The time had come when Britain was no longer prepared to trade with China entirely on Chinese terms.

As the general mood became uglier, the British residents at Canton, who had already retreated from Canton to Macao, decided to retreat still further, to the virtually barren island of Hong Kong. In the interim, the astute James Matheson was doing more opium business than ever. Prices in India had collapsed because of the actions of Commissioner Lin, providing a wonderful buying opportunity, while demand for the drug was undiminished. It was just a matter of supplying through new centres, such as Manila in the Philippines.

In June 1840 the British armed steamer *Madagascar*, together with three 74-gun ships of the line – the *Wellesley*, the *Blenheim* and the *Melville* – arrived off Canton. However, this port was not the agreed strategic target. Instead, it was decided to blockade Chusan, some 1,300 kilometres further up the coast and significantly

Left: The Praya Grande on the Peninsula of Macao, mid-19th century, by a Chinese artist. The Portuguese were the first Europeans to arrive in China, in 1517, and they established a base at Macao. Later it became a favoured resort of Westerners of all nations. (Martyn Gregory Gallery, London.)

A Chinese war junk by a Chinese artist, mid-19th century. These junks proved no match for the British warships such as the Nemesis. *(National Maritime Museum, London.)*

nearer to Peking (Beijing), where, it was felt, the attack would make more of an impression on the emperor. Tinghai was duly taken and four war junks were shot to pieces in short order. In the face of this reverse, Commissioner Lin was promptly removed from power and an experienced Chinese diplomat called Kishen was instructed to sue for peace. Negotiations, however, proved to be protracted. For a start Kishen insisted that they take place in Canton, which was the scene of the original problem, rather than at Chusan where the British fleet was now based. And even when Canton was agreed upon, Kishen continued to procrastinate.

Meanwhile, the armed paddle-steamer *Nemesis* entered into the fray. The *Nemesis* was of a new construction along novel lines. Built by the company John Laird entirely from iron, it was 56 metres long and only 8.8 metres wide, and was equipped with a rocket launcher and two very large guns. It had been dispatched from Britain under conditions of great secrecy. Although not a regular British Navy warship, it had Admiralty letters of marque which permitted it to destroy enemy shipping. The most unique feature of the *Nemesis* was its flat bottom and extremely shallow draught of only 1.8 metres. This meant that it could, if required, penetrate upriver and inflict serious damage on inland fortifications and towns. However, while the *Nemesis* might have been advanced as a warship, its sailing qualities were poor and on more than

164

one occasion it nearly foundered on the voyage out. At one point a large split appeared in the ironwork of its hull. However, emergency repairs were successfully carried out and it finally appeared off Macao on 25 November 1840. By January 1841 Elliot, the British Superintendent of Trade, had grown tired of the continual delays in negotiating a treaty with Kishen and he ordered his warships in to attack the Chinese forts along the Pearl River. The *Nemesis* took part in the attack and the result was devastating. Chinese defences were smashed and the Chinese naval commander, Admiral Kuan, was killed.

The cultural gap between the two adversaries is graphically brought home by comparing the *Nemesis*, a product of the Industrial Revolution, built of iron and powered by steam, with the traditional war junks of the Chinese, still reliant on oar and sail and completely lacking in effective armaments. Ironically, there were certain aspects of the *Nemesis* design that had startling similarities with the junk tradition of shipbuilding. For instance, the afore-mentioned flat-bottomed hull enabled it to negotiate shallow rivers. It was also one of the very first Western ships to use transverse bulkheads, which had been in use in the East for many hundreds of years.

Chinese swords captured during the first Opium War. (National Maritime Museum, London.)

This illustration shows Lieutenant Douglas, who was a prisoner of war in China in 1840. Images such as this were used to stir up anti-Chinese feeling among the British at home, during the first Opium War. (National Maritime Museum, London.)

But as a machine of destruction the *Nemesis* was in a completely different class from the junks that confronted it. Faced with the overwhelming superiority of the British fleet, it is hardly surprising that Kishen procrastinated no longer. The Chuenpi Convention was hastily signed, by which Britain was to receive $6 million in compensation, the island of Hong Kong was to be ceded to British control, and in future there was to be equality of status between nationals – instead of the infuriating

View of the Jardine Matheson building at Hong Kong, by M. Bruce, 1846. After the British acquired Hong Kong, the firm of Jardine Matheson used it as a successful trading base for opium and other commodities. (National Maritime Museum, London.)

business of British ambassadors having to kow-tow to representatives of the emperor.

As treaties go, this one was particularly short-lived. Lord Palmerston, the Foreign Secretary, was most unhappy with the terms that had been agreed. As far as he was concerned, Hong Kong was nothing but a barren island and, as a minimum, he wanted trading rights at three important ports along the Chinese coast, and significantly more in the way of compensation. Not only had the costs of the seized

A portrait of the Imperial Commissioner Ch'iying, who was responsible for ratifying the Treaty of Nanking. Chinese artist, mid-19th century. (Martyn Gregory Gallery, London.)

opium to be recovered but also the expenses of the entire expedition. The general sentiment back home was pretty much in accordance with the views expressed by the young Queen Victoria:

All we wanted might have been got if it had not been for the unaccountably strange conduct of Charles Elliot, who completely disobeyed his instructions and tried to get the lowest terms he could.

Kishen fared even worse than his British opposite number. When the emperor heard the terms he had conceded, he was arrested and brought back to Peking in chains. At least Elliot had the dignity of a decent berth on the voyage home.

A reinforced British fleet and a further contingent of troops, under the command of Sir William Parker and Sir Henry Pottinger, set out up the Chinese coast a second time, with the aim, on this occasion, of blockading the Yangtse itself. The Chinese warships were again simply no match for the British. Chinese

armaments generally still belonged to the era of the Middle Ages, their troops employing chain-mail, bows and arrows and poor-quality gunpowder. In the Treaty of Nanking which followed, in August 1842, the Chinese agreed to pay $21 million in compensation, opened up five ports to British trade, conceded the issue of British subjects being answerable only to British law, and the ceding of Hong Kong was ratified. However, once again nothing was said about opium traffic. The trade in opium was not formally legalised by the Chinese until 1858 and only then because of continued pressure from the West. But from 1842 onwards China was effectively opened up to the Western trading powers, a state which lasted until the Communist revolution of 1949, when it was abruptly closed again.

It has been argued that Britain went to war with China not primarily to enforce its right to sell opium to the Chinese, but because China's economy was languishing under a medieval system of ineffective centralised controls, headed by a largely defunct imperial regime. From this perspective it becomes historically inevitable that China should have been bullied and cajoled into the 'virtues' of nineteenth-century liberal free trade. However, from the viewpoint of a Western society in the twenty-first century, itself ravaged by drug abuse, it is difficult to take quite such a historically complacent attitude. Would today's Western political leaders stand up for the rights of foreign drug barons to import heroin and cocaine into the USA and Europe under the banner of free trade? In the end, Captain Pearl and all those on the *Tek Sing* were caught up in historical processes which are still being played out.

Above: The signing of the Treaty of Nanking by which Hong Kong was ceded to Britain, five ports were to be opened up to foreign traders, and China was to pay $21 million compensation. (Painted by Captain John Platt, 1846, National Maritime Museum, London.)

Left: The soldier's mess, Canton, by Lieutenant John Meade of the Royal Marines, c. 1858. The painting shows French and British troops quartered in a Chinese temple at the start of the second Opium War. (Martyn Gregory Gallery, London.)

Glossary

NAUTICAL

Barque Usually a sailing-vessel with three masts, square rigged on the fore and main masts, with a fore and aft rig on the stern mast.

Bhandarry A low-caste Indian, originating from the Bombay region, commonly found among a lascar (see below) crew.

Budgerow An Indian vessel, of a barge-like construction, with no keel, used mainly for transporting passengers along the higher reaches of rivers.

Country ship A ship used for trading between different ports of the East, particularly between India and China, rather than undertaking the long-haul voyages between Europe and America and China and India.

Dhow A vessel commonly found in the Indian Ocean and the Eastern seas, of Arabic origin, usually with one mast and a lateen rig.

Gudgeon A metal ring fixed to the sternpost of a ship into which the pin or pintle, (see below), of the rudder is inserted so that the rudder can swing freely in whichever direction it is moved by the tiller. A minimum of two gudgeons and two pintles is required to hang a rudder.

Hydrographer A person who surveys the seas, establishing the outline of coasts, the depths of the waters, and the positions of reefs and rocks, in order to assist safe navigation.

Lascar An Indian crew member. European ships came to be manned increasingly by lascars during the eighteenth and nineteenth centuries.

Lee side The side of a ship or island which is sheltered or protected from the wind.

Nachoda The master or captain of a native ship, a term widely used throughout the East.

Pintle The metal pin attached to a rudder which is slotted into the gudgeon (see above) so that the rudder can be hung from the sternpost of the ship.

Prahu Small Malaysian vessels often used with outriggers and with unusually shaped lateen sails.

Sampan Small, light Chinese vessels with a shallow draught and sometimes a single sail, used in harbours and coastal areas for loading larger junks, selling produce, and miscellaneous short-distance transport.

Seacunny The steersman in a lascar crew.

Serang An Indian term for the chief of a lascar (see above) crew.

Shoal water Shallow water where a ship is in danger of running aground.

Slop clothing Clothing issued by the British Navy to its sailors, which came to mean, more generally, any clothing doled out to one while on board ship.

Supercargo The most important merchant on board a trading ship.

Tindal The equivalent of a petty officer in a lascar (see above) crew.

Topass A low-ranking Portuguese-Indian, often found as a member of a lascar (see above) crew.

Left: One of a pair of stone lions found aboard the Tek Sing. *They were used by the Chinese to ward off evil spirits. (Nagel Auctions, Stuttgart.)*

171

VOC The abbreviation of Verenigde Oostindische Compagnie, which means the United East India Company, the name given to the Dutch East India Company founded in 1602.

Wale A longitudinal, structurally reinforcing piece of wood, running around the outside of the hull in the general area of the waterline or above.

Wangkang A name often used for large seagoing junks that originate from Canton.

Weather side The side of a ship or an island against which the wind blows or which is most exposed to the wind.

PORCELAIN

Blanc de chine Translucent white porcelain, largely produced at Dehua.

Blue-and-white Painted on the white or near white body with blue decoration, which is then covered with a colourless or near colourless glaze.

Celadon A glaze first developed in the Song period and coloured various shades of green.

Kaolin A very pure form of white china clay.

Knop The knob on the top of a bowl cover.

Monochrome A single uniform colour.

Petuntse Feldspathic rock used in the making of porcelain.

Swatow ware A kind of porcelain typified by red, green and yellow colours added on top of the glaze, sometimes with a blue underglaze.

Vitreous Glass-like.

CHINESE DRUGS

Bezoar A concretion found in the stomachs of various animals and caused by diseases in those animals. Much prized as a medicine, particularly those obtained from Persian goats which traditionally fetched ten times their weight in gold.

Camphor Camphor was one of the most valued items in the Chinese pharmacopoeia. True camphor was an aromatic oil or gum obtained from a tree that grew only in the islands of Sumatra and Borneo and then only between the equator and the third degree north. It was obtained by going into the forests, cutting down the camphor trees (*Dryobalanops camphora*) and scraping the crystals from the fissures of the wood. Only one in ten of the camphor trees yielded any of the drug and so its collection was a difficult and painstaking process. The trees could not be cultivated but grew only in the wild. The true camphor of Sumatra and Borneo, known as Baroos camphor, was to be carefully distinguished from the product of the more common camphor tree (*Laurus camphora*), which was a member of the laurel family, and which grew widely throughout China, Japan and Taiwan. Camphor was used by the Chinese mainly as a topical application on swellings, bruises and cuts as well as for skin infections.

Cassia Cassia comes in three forms. There is the large cassia tree, *Laurus cassia*, that grows commonly in China, the bark of which is called *cassia lignea* and is used as an aromatic, similar to but less pungent than cinnamon. Then there is the plant, *Cassia fistula*, which produces pods, also known as senna pods. And finally there are what are called cassia buds, which are supposedly the berries of the cassia tree but which according to some authorities actually come from the cinnamon tree.

China root The root of the *Smilax China*, a climbing plant, thickly jointed and knobbly, reddish brown on the outside and a pale, glittering red within.

Dragon's blood The exotic-sounding 'dragon's blood' was held in high regard by the Chinese. It was, rather disappointingly, not dragon's blood, or the blood of any creature remotely similar to a dragon, but a secretion from a species of large rattan, the *Calamus rotang*, which grew in Borneo and Sumatra. It was gathered in oval drops or 'tears' which were translucent when held up to the light and crimson in colour when powdered, thus the name. As well as being used as a medicine, it was also used in painting and as a varnish.

Ginseng The dried root of the *Panax quinquefolium*. The word ginseng means, in Chinese, 'in the shape of a man'. A widely consumed cure-all in China, which, though native to Tartary, from the eighteenth century was also grown in Canada and North America, from where it was exported in large quantities to China.

Musk The secretion of the deer, which collected in a small pouch of skin, about the size of a walnut. Good musk was of a dark purplish colour, dry and light in weight, and very expensive. Because of its high price the purchaser had to be wary of counterfeit products. The purity was best tested by placing a small amount of the musk in a glass of wine to which it would impart a strong scent if it was the genuine article.

Rhubarb The root of the rhubarb plant, which was dug up in the early spring, cut into long, flat pieces and thoroughly dried by hanging them up in the shade. If it became damp during the drying process, the rhubarb was ruined. The price was about forty dollars per hundredweight and it was generally believed that the very best rhubarb came from Turkey or Russia, although it was also widely grown in China. It was used as a cure for both diarrhoea and constipation, the effect depending on the quantity administered. It was usually shipped in its 'garbled' state, by which was meant that it had been treated and refined to free it of all impurities.

Star anise The produce of a small aromatic tree, *Illicium anisatum*, that grows in China. The reddish-coloured pods are about a centimetre long and joined at one end to form a star shape. Both the pods and their white seeds can be chewed, the seeds being sweeter but less scented. Used by the Chinese both to season sweet dishes and as a medicine.

THE MOST IMPORTANT CHINESE DYNASTIES

Qin	221–207 BC
Han	206 BC–AD 220
Age of Division	220–589
Sui	589–618
Tang	618–906
Five Dynasties Period	906–960
Song	960–1277
Yuan	1277–1368
Ming	1368–1644
Manchu Qing or Ching	1644–1911

MISCELLANEOUS

Arrack An alcoholic drink fermented from a mixture of molasses, the juice of the cocoa-nut or palm tree, and rice.

Baboos A term used by the English to denote wealthy Indians.

Behar Also spelt Bihar. The region in the north-east part of India where the bulk of the opium was produced during the British colonial period.

Button Different coloured and shaped buttons on the crests of Chinese caps were used to denote a mandarin's rank.

Campong The Chinese quarter of a town.

Confucius (551–479 BC) China's first moral philosopher, who emphasised the importance of filial piety and the responsibility rulers had towards the common people. He helped establish the Chinese tradition of the scholar-administrator.

Factory A warehouse and place of business for the European and American merchant community, each nation having their own factory in the different trading ports. Also sometimes used as living quarters.

Kittysol A parasol made from bamboo and paper, and a frequent item of export.

Nankeen A tough, yellow-coloured cotton, produced in the Nanking area, and very popular in Britain for trousers in the nineteenth century.

Selected Bibliography

PRINTED SOURCES

JOURNALS AND NEWSPAPERS (VARIOUS EDITIONS)
Amoy Gazetteer
Bataviasche Courant
Bengal Directory
Calcutta Journal
Canton Register
Chinese Repository
London Illustrated News
Madras Courier

BOOKS
Abel, C. *Narrative of a journey in the interior of China...*, London 1818
Alexander, W. *The costume of China*, London 1805
Anon. *Description of the Chinese junk* Keying, London 1848
Barrow, J. *Travels in China*, London 1804
Crawfurd, J. *History of the Indian Archipelago*, 3 volumes, London 1820
Crawfurd, J. *A descriptive dictionary of the Indian Islands...*, London 1856
Daniell, T. and W. *A picturesque voyage to India; by the way of China*, London 1810
Davis, J.F. *The Chinese*, 2 volumes, London 1836
Davis, J.F. *Sketches of China*, 2 volumes, London 1841
Earl, G. *The eastern seas*, London 1837
Forbes, Robert. *Letters from China 1838–1840*, Mystic 1996

Fraser, J. *Views of Calcutta*, London 1824
Gutzlaff, K. *Journal of three voyages along the coast of China in 1831, 1832 and 1833*, London 1834
McLeod, J. *Voyage of His Majesty's Ship Alceste*, London 1818
Marsden, W. *The history of Sumatra*, London 1783
Medhurst, W.H. *Hokkien dialect*, Macao 1832
Medhurst, W.H. *Chinese miscellany*, 4 volumes in 1, Shanghai 1849–50
Milburn, W. *Oriental commerce*, London 1813
Nieuhof, J. *An embassy...*, London 1669
Ong, Tae-hae. *The Chinaman abroad*, Shanghai 1849
Phipps, J. *A guide to the commerce of Bengal*, Calcutta 1823
Raffles, T.S. *The history of Java*, 2 volumes, London 1817
Staunton, G.T. *Miscellaneous notices relating to China*, London 1825–50
Wathen, J. *Journal of a voyage, in 1811 and 1812, to Madras and China*, London 1814
Wright, G.N. *China in a series of views*, drawings by Thomas Allom, 1843

MODERN WORKS

BOOKS AND ARTICLES
Audemard, L. *Les jonques Chinoises*, Rotterdam 1957
Blusse, Leonard. *Strange company*,

Dordrecht, Holland 1986

Brindley, H.H. 'The *Keying*', *Mariner's Mirror*, volume 8, 1922

Cameron, Nigel. *Barbarians and mandarins*, Oxford 1989

Donnelly, I.A. 'Foochow pole junks', *Mariner's Mirror*, volume 9, 1923

Donnelly, I.A. 'Early Chinese ships and trade', *Mariner's Mirror*, volume 11, 1925

Dukes, E.J. *Everyday life in China or scenes in Fuh-kien*, London 1885

Fay, Peter. *The opium war*, North Carolina 1975

Greenberg, Michael. *British trade and the opening of China 1800–1842*, Cambridge 1951

Gungwu, Wang. 'The Nanhai trade', *Journal of the Malayan Branch of the Royal Asiatic Society*, volume 31, 1958

Janin, H. *The India–China opium trade in the nineteenth century*, London 1999

Jorg, C.J.A. *Porcelain and the Dutch China trade*, The Hague 1982

Levathes, Louise. *When China ruled the seas*, Oxford 1996

Lohanda, Mona. *The Kapitan Cina of Batavia 1837–1942*, Indonesia

Lubbock, Basil. *The opium clippers*, Boston 1933

Mills, J.V.G. *Ma Huan*, Cambridge 1970

Mills, J.V.G. 'Chinese navigators', *Archipel 18*, 1979

Morse, H.B. *The chronicles of the East India Company trading to China 1635–1834*, 5 volumes, Oxford 1926

Mulder, W.Z. 'Wu Pei charts', *T'oung Pao*, volume 37

Nair, Thankappan (ed.) *Calcutta in the 19th century*, Calcutta 1989

Needham, Joseph. *Science and civilisation in China*, 4 volumes, Cambridge 1954–71

Orange, J. *The Chater Collection*, pictures relating to China, 1924

Parkinson, C.N. *Trade in the Eastern seas 1793–1813*, Cambridge 1937

Ptak, R. *China's seaborne trade with South and Southeast Asia*, Aldershot 1999

Purcell, Victor. *The Chinese in Southeast Asia*, London 1951

Reid, A. *South East Asia in the early modern era*, Ithaca, NY 1993

Rockhill, W.W. 'Chinese trade with the Eastern Archipelago', *T'oung Pao*, volumes 15 and 16

Singh, Narayan. *The East India Company's monopoly industries 1773–1833*, Bihar 1980

Steinberg, D.J. *In search of Southeast Asia*, Sydney 1987

Trocki, Carl. *Opium and empire*, Ithaca, NY 1990

Van Leur, J.C. *Indonesian trade and society*, The Hague 1955

Wakeman, Frederic. *Conflict and control in late imperial China*, Berkeley

Wakeman, Frederic. *Strangers at the gate*, Berkeley 1966

Waley, Arthur. *The opium war through Chinese eyes*, London 1958

FURTHER READING ON THE PORCELAIN

Donnelly, P.J. *Blanc de Chine*, Frederick A. Praeger: New York 1969

Jianzhong Chen. *Dehua folk blue and white wares*, Cultural Relics Publishing House: China 1999

Lo, K.S. *The stonewares of Yixing from the Ming period to the present day*, Sotheby Publications: Hong Kong 1986

South East Asia Ceramic Society, *Nonya ware and Kitchen Ch'ing*. Malaysia 1981

Tek Sing Treasures, sale catalogue, Nagel Auctions: Stuttgart 2000.

Acknowledgements

I would like to thank the following for their help in writing and producing this book: Steve McNamara of Ocean Salvage Corporation; David Judell; Aaron Playle; everyone at Book Production Consultants plc, but in particular Colin Walsh, Tim McPhee, Roz Williams and Sue Gray; Marcus Fletcher for his editing skills; Martyn Gregory Gallery for their patience in the supply of transparencies; Dave Moran of *Dive New Zealand Magazine* for his excellent photographs; Nigel Orloff of Masks, Images in Motion for his equally excellent photographs; everyone at Nagel Auctions, Stuttgart, but in particular Robin Straub, Uwe Jourdan and Michael Trautmann; all the divers, technicians and crew involved in the salvage but in particular Trevor McEniry, Abdul Rahim and Arrasan Sundaram; David Freedman for his very informative contribution on the porcelain; Ros Pickford for her unfailing support and helpful suggestions; and, of course, Mike Hatcher for his unflagging enthusiasm and ability to make things happen.

Further Information

For further information on the discovery and
salvage of the *Tek Sing* and also on the sale of its porcelain
cargo see the following web sites:

Tek-sing.de
Teksing.com
Treasureshipdiscovery.com
auction.de
OceanSalvage.com.au